# Awaking Spirit

## reclamation of being

### Autobiography and Teachings of

### Keith Joseph Chouinard

### Uncovering Lies of Illusion

When you are embroiled within lies
their attachments to your reality cause illusion.
When you clear away the veils
the light burns away the illusions for all to see.

The harder one pushes a lie
The harder one tries to cover the truth
The harder in return the light shines through
The truth is always seen
The attachments do not exist
Living within the light is freedom
KJC

# Awaking Spirit, reclamation of being

Copyright © 2012 Keith Joseph Chouinard

All Rights Reserved

This book may not be reproduced in whole or in part, by any means, electronic or mechanical, without prior written permission from the author, except for brief passages in connection with a review.

For Information, or to order additional copies of this book, please contact:

www.AwakingSpirit.com


Cover Intellectual Concept Design by: Keith Joseph Chouinard
Illustrated by: Ralph Masiello

Typeset in:
Title Font: Eras Light ITC
Body Font: Calibri
Memories: Calibri Italic

Editing Help: Elizabeth, Peggy, and Jodie

Comma Enforcement Officer: Peggy

---

This book is dedicated to overcoming fear

*'Fears Ascending*

# Awaking Spirit, reclamation of being

**A special note from the editing help:**

We have noticed during the editing of these pages an Old English Language or also referred to as Anglo-Saxon.

Earliest period dates to the fifth century A.D. The language was split in three periods within a timeline throughout history.

We must look carefully to find the resemblance between Keith's words and our modern English of today.

We ask the reader to consider reading this book slower than they may be pressed to do within the excitement of the materials content.

Keith would suggest taking plenty of breaks from reading to process your ego, judgment, personality, opinion and moving your learned knowledge aside to consider what is actually being said within the multidimensional realms of this material.

We apologize for any alterations of the meanings of Keith's words by our encouragement of punctuation and grammar changes and hope in future editions Keith will be able to correct any mistakes from our work.

Remember to BREATHE -

## CHAPTERS:

My Introduction .................................................................. 9

Multidimensional Memories ............................................. 15

Just Because Others Cannot Make Sense of You Does Not Mean That You Are Senseless ............................................ 47

Colorado ............................................................................ 69

Massachusetts .................................................................. 93

Turning Eighteen ............................................................. 121

The Violet Flame Awakening .......................................... 139

The Descent .................................................................... 149

On My Own for Real ....................................................... 163

Turning $50 into a Business and Hiding in Ambition .......... 171

A New Chapter Begins.................................................... 193

Reiki is Love ................................................................... 205

Holding Space during the Passing of Others ................. 217

THC Stands for "The Holistic Center" ............................ 231

Glastonbury is calling .................................................... 239

Runaway out West ......................................................... 249

Past Lives Becoming Present Life .................................. 263

The Future is NOW ......................................................... 285

# Foreword

This is a book about developing the courage and learning to BE love by stepping out of fear and illusion. Many whom consider themselves to be on a spiritual path, eventually discover that humans are multidimensional beings. Every person has a purpose of being on the planet at this time. Although we may each have different vocations, or choice of lifestyles, we are here to awaken ourself and one another to the promised "age of peace". We do this by simply being who we TRULY are.

In this book, as well as through his beingness, Keith helps the reader recognize that our true nature is to be love, loving and peaceful in all situations. There is light in even the darkest moments when one is able to view the moment through the eyes of love. Within any darkness there are opportunities to learn lessons that eventually lead us into light.

Through Keith's story, the reader can learn how paralyzing fear can be. Fear can hold us back from realizing our true nature, and how to express our true self out into the world.

Keith is one who can experience other dimensions, while simultaneously being awake in the third dimension. Keith was born into this life with a beautiful gift. However, because of the lack of awareness that many people have, he grew to believe that there was something wrong with him. He was "different", or so he and others thought. However, he is not so different. He is simply one of the blessed few who can easily move through multiple dimensions simultaneously and was born knowing his true self.

This book has broad appeal, as many people have had experiences that could not be explained through "normal" levels of awareness. In order to "fit in" with the mainstream, those of us who have had those experiences may have chosen to hide from them.

Keith writes about seeing into his own future, and at times fearing what he saw. The fear was due to the lack of understanding, in the moment, that indeed there is light contained in every experience. This is a book that can help the reader to look to the other side of uncomfortable experiences and to let the light shine fully from their heart. As the heart light illumines the darkness, we have the opportunity to remember who we are and why we are incarnate on the earth at this time.

I am grateful to Keith for claiming the courage to BE a guiding light of love for all who are blessed to read this book and to know Keith's true self.

Love, peace and infinite blessings,

Laurelle Shanti Gaia, President
Infinite Light Healing Studies Center, Inc.
Sedona, Arizona, USA

infinitelight.com and laurellegaia.com

# MY INTRODUCTION

**M**emories as a child for me deal with psychically seeing into many parts of my life before it even took place.

As a small child I had visions which gave me awareness into thirty and forty or more years of my life. I have come to realize that I may have even seen into what appears to be my past lives while dealing with being a child within this current stream of life.

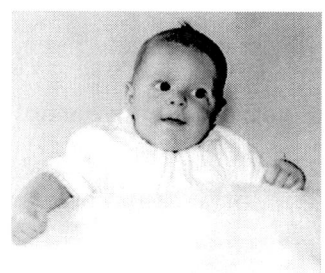

**Baby Keith**

I live a very multidimensional life of awareness. I sit here typing at age forty seven, writing a book I knew I would write many years ago. I sensed others knew I would write books as well. Though some of those people aware of me back then I suspect may not have comprehended what the books would really be about. They did not comprehend how their interactions with me would not only affect the books I would later write, but as well the man I would become.

I needed to learn to become even more sensory aware to overcome the reactions of others within my life and learn to discern light from their own diseases of consciousness. Spirit would teach me many things within the realms of light.

Darkness also would hide me from those who would want to control me for their own motives by looking into my aura and destiny while creating a prophecy of their own making.

Escaping into the darkness had its own perils. In losing my conscious connection to spirit I would be adrift within the reactions and horrors of mankind. I would be buffeted by the grace of god forever finding my way back into the arms and light of spirit.

I was told that in a future space of time an era of light would arrive for all and I could become present once again without fear.

I would become part of a family of spirit beings, who by spirit presence held the space and light of free will as they overcame the hypnotic illusion and entrainment of the false reality that they were mere human beings.

The human race would awaken to the full realities that they indeed were spiritual beings portraying themselves as human. In the age of awaking spirit, the reclamation of being would transform the pains of humanity into the light of truth and unconditional love would thrive.

**We are spiritual beings of light.**

My name in this lifetime is Keith Joseph Chouinard. I was born in Springfield, Massachusetts within the United States of America on August $8^{th}$, 1964. I have French and Irish ancestry within me, and I am told I also have Native American descendants.

As I write this book, I reside in the small town of West Brookfield, Massachusetts. My job title is complex for the uninitiated. While I currently serve as the non-profit director of a wellness center called, "The Holistic Center" it could be said that I am an empathic therapist.

As an empathic therapist, I work to discern and see, sense, feel other peoples energy fields when they come to me. I see spirits at times and have visions of things to come or things that have happened within the past. Throughout history, people had called those like me: Mystics, Seers, Shamans, Witches, Sorcerers, and even Christians.

Possibly I should back up some and not get ahead of the story, or myself for who I am. I will offer what I have learned to discern at this moment in what is called time, within the framework of what is accepted by mainstream society, as it is in the beginning of this year 2012 on the planet we call Earth.

You may be starting to sense a pattern here that is developing. It is part of what makes me uniquely me, and I hope as you read further into this you will as well sense the pattern that makes you uniquely you. I hope for you to be able to become more aware of the multidimensionality of your own being.

**This book is dedicated to overcoming fear.**

This book is written for those people that are hiding in fear from their own awareness of the greatness for whom they truly are. We are spiritual beings coming forth from the higher realms into the $3^{rd}$ dimension having a human experience.

Once we overcome our fears, as well as the fears of others that we may not knowingly realize or feel are indeed being energetically imprinted upon our states of consciousness, we can open to the truth and the light of love as to what is real. As we do this our own light of vision increases and we can comprehend what has been in front of us all along within the realm of our spirits.

Society lost much of their connection to their souls when they started to believe that they were human beings as opposed to the fact that they are indeed spiritual beings, being human. Language is an interesting thing which if we are not careful we can get lost within it.

I have heard it said that the Hebrew language is a language based on mathematics. The easiest way to understand this for me is when, the Hebrew word for man and the Hebrew word for woman are translated into their numerical values. When you then add those two numbers together the number you have then found, from the combination of the other two, can then be translated into the Hebrew word for child.

I believe the purity of a language is in the ability of it being able to connect one energetic thought into a stream of connecting thoughts that then have an energetic meaning when combined together. The purity of connecting with others is within the ability of a person to clearly speak their truths and communicate from the heart in a way that honors the person being communicated with as well as the person doing the communication.

The universe is one big mathematical equation and I believe that it keeps on giving. The more we go with the flow of being and allow our lives to be a co-creation of love we clear away the confusion that blocks the flow of life and the more life gives to us.

**One of the statements I would make to people when I became more open was:**

*"I am an empath, which means I can see/sense and feel energy fields, not only of people, but other things as well. I see spirits, from passed on relatives or friends of people to people's spirit guides and even spirits from higher and lower realms. Yes, that means I*

*actually have sensed/seen demons and entities/energies lacking much light. But I have also seen and experienced things that I would have to describe as angels and souls from the higher realms of light."*

**I would go on to tell people if they were still listening that:**

*"You as well are an empath, for everyone is. The difference is that some people absorb so much of the energy of others that they are not able to sense which are their feelings coming from within themselves, as opposed to what are the feelings and energies or even thoughts of others around them. Then there is the other spectrum of those that put off themselves so much of their own energy, that others without clear energetic boundaries are oppressed by them and they themselves are not able to sense where others may begin and their own energetic boundaries stop."*

**One of my favorite phrases *is: "to work with our processes"***

That is what I believe we must do, "to work with our process," if we want to better understand what we are feeling and sensing within this life.

Learning to overcome our reactions to find that space of being that simply "is" from the moment we are born, to the moment we pass on within the next journey into knowing, is learning how to know who we really are. If you do not know your own being can you effectively know another?

Many people attempt to go outside of themselves to create a life. It seems to me that the more we take the path within and learn to co-create with the universe, the more we are given from those results and experiences, the more that the universe offers us grace of being in return.

For many this book may read as outlandish and made up fiction or possibly even the ravings of someone psychotic and indeed even a megalomaniac.

I have been cautioned by some to write this veiled as fiction so as to not draw so much attention to myself, or even so I do not sound "full of myself".

This book is the story of my life; it is an autobiography written with memories and teachings of things I have learned to discern. My hopes in writing this, is that others living in fear or pain and hiding from their own truths can go within while reading this book and allow it to actually be about finding their own being. I hope this book will assist in bringing forward your true essence within the presence of learning to hold the space of light. For I believe we are truly one within the light of love and we are family.

As each of us work with our processes, we raise within the ascension of the consciousness of light. Not only do we ascend, but those around us - including those within the other realms of spirit, are lifted to greater heights of awareness and being, of the ascended spirit family that we are.

# Anye (ahn yay)

## Aligning Heaven and Earth

Courtesy of: BePeaceNow.org

# Multidimensional Memories

When I started telling this story of my life, of life within these pages, I spoke of memories. My memories of this current lifetime go back to before I could even walk.

> I can remember being in my crib and wanting so bad to be able to be out of it, walking around like everyone else. I can remember being a baby and held by my mother, at the kitchen sink, as she lovingly washed me. I can remember seeing and feeling her concerns that I was safe as she cleaned me, I knew I was deeply loved by her.

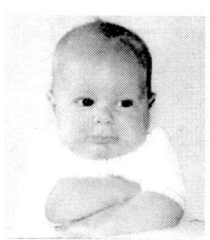

I have vague, but distinct memories, of being in my crib as a baby and having my spirit guides speak to my concerns of the many things I felt and my desires to move on with my life.

> It was difficult to be a baby and to have no control over anything. I was fully dependent on the people around me, and these people often seemed unaware of what was actually going on.

**I needed to wait to grow and learn to gain my own self- control, and gain my independence, within the space of time.**

> I watched everything going on around me curious as to how I seemed much more aware of the things taking place, than most of those around me. I seem to remember

*understanding much of what was being said though I had no ability to make sense of how to speak physically myself.*

*Some of the other children scared me at times. There were moments when they made noise and even though my mother seemed to understand them, the noise or words made no sense to me. I was confused as to what was going on around me.*

Spirit attempted to quiet me by explaining what was going on and that someday I would understand more, but I just wanted to be past that stage of life.

**My earliest memories of my father are not many.**

*The earliest time I can remember of my father, was sitting at the kitchen table at the apartment we lived in on Summer Street. He was playing what I would later learn in life was a game of cards with his friends. I can remember wanting to get his attention, but he was busy and I was told that I needed to behave myself. Somewhere within that memory I can feel that I loved him, and he may have played with me at times, but sadly, I cannot recall those times.*

The only other time that I can recall of my father, from childhood, is a strange memory that until fifteen years ago I thought was a memory of my older brother for he didn't feel like a father to me in those memories.

*I can recall vividly that we were getting dressed to go outside for a walk somewhere, as if it were a mission. It was going to be getting dark soon and I could hear and sense some disturbance from my sister and brothers as to if I was going to be able to do this, since I hadn't been walking for*

> very long, and that for me it would be a good distance to go.
>
> It was said that it would be good for me and that it would strengthen my legs and make me strong. I can remember vividly crossing the crosswalk in the middle of North Brookfield, Massachusetts on foot being terrified cars might come at any point. I wanted to be picked up and held instead of walking.
>
> We walked down the next street to the corner, which seemed like a very long walk to me.

As an adult I have walked down that same street and find it curious how what is an easy five minute walk as an adult would seem to take so long as a child with so much determination.

> In my memory, we were now standing at the corner of this street. I was holding the hand of this taller guy who would then let go and tell the other boys to go to the house that he pointed to. He wanted them to look within the windows to see what was going on in there.
>
> My mother, he said was there. He wanted to know what she was doing. He claimed that we would never see her again that she didn't love us anymore. I recall the other boys yelling, due to the fact they didn't want to do as he said. It felt like he threatened them somehow and they ran off and did as he demanded.
>
> I remember the boys returning and stating what they saw. There were more disagreements and then, in my memory, the long sad walk home. It felt like this was not the way it was supposed to be and how could it be this way?

For some reason, as I have recalled this memory in earlier stages of my life, it didn't dawn on me till about fifteen years ago that the taller guy in the memory was actually my dad.

As I mentioned before, in my earlier recollections of the memory, I transferred one of my brothers as being my dad and didn't even realize that my father was actually part of that memory.

When it finally dawned on me that it indeed was my dad and not my brother the shock was profound to me in realizing how much he must not have felt like a father to me even back then.

> *Shortly after this experience my mother reappears in my memories, she indeed did love me. In fact, I would learn many years later that she had battled for custody of me and my siblings, for six weeks, to get us back. Up until then I was led to believe I would never see her again because she did not love me.*
>
> *Though, now my father disappears from my memories for me to be led to believe, he did not love me. My oldest brother leaves as well, and my mother brings with her a new man. The brother I am left with now, warns me about this new man coming into my life. I am told he is to replace my father and I am not sure what to believe.*

I can remember memories of fear. Are we safe? What is going to happen? What did actually happen? Why is everything in such turmoil in life? I am in the beginning stages of my life and it is hard enough. Why do all these people around me not understand the confusion and pain they are causing, do they not know how to behave properly?

**Life felt very hard for me as a small child.**

Most people were very scary to me. Just being around others was painful enough, but when they opened their mouths the things they said, I could often tell, were lies. There were so many words that just felt painful to hear even if I did not know their meanings.

There were times I would have to interact with adults and was expected to behave in a certain way, when I could see straight through them. I learned that I was not allowed to let on what I was actually seeing since they were much bigger than me. They believed they were in control.

I now had to deal with this new man in the life of my mother and I was fearful I would lose part of her in the process. When in fact, I knew, I was going to lose much of her in the process I just didn't know how to deal with it or what I could do about it. It was hard enough surviving from all the pain I felt around me and the fact I would have to grow up and deal with this big world around me that felt so full of discord and pain.

With the new man in my mother's life, came new brothers and sisters. We were told we would be meeting them soon and that at least one of them would be moving in with us. Of everything happening up to now, with this big change to the family, this seemed like something good may come of the whole experience yet.

> *The night my new brother came over was caught on movie film. It was one of those older style film cameras that you would then watch the movie on big reels of film. We sat by the door, waiting for him to come in. We heard him come up the stairs and just as soon as he walked through the*

> door, being caught live on film, he saw my older brother and recognized him as the boy at school that bullied him.
>
> No sooner than he walked in the door, he turned round in fright and ran away.

What stands out to me in my memories is that this new brother was the one family member in my life that actually behaved like family. He treated me like a brother without judgment or scorn and has helped me the best he could throughout his life in ways he doesn't even realize.

During this time period many things happened. As I had stated previously being around most people was a very hard thing for me to do.

> There was a day I was outside playing by myself. I decided that I was a big enough boy to be able to cross the street alone. I built up the courage to do that and went to the little store across the street to see if I could buy candy.
>
> As I entered, the owner that I had seen before was at the counter speaking with an older boy. The owner said hello and from the conversation I overheard, it sounded like the older boy was either on school break from a college, or was about to start college. He was at an age the store owner made a big deal about.
>
> The owner of the store asked me what I wanted to be when I grew up. I was a little shy and didn't really say anything in reply, so the owner and the older boy came over and started talking to me.
>
> The older boy decided he was going to buy me a frozen ice pop and told me to pick the flavor. There seemed to be

some hidden interest in which color or flavor that I would choose, more so than it would make sense to be.

The man and the boy seemed like they were up to something. There was discussion of some course the boy was in or what he wanted to do for a profession. It seemed to me, as I look back with an adult frame of reference, that he was planning on being a psychiatrist of some sort. It seemed like some of the conversation had that time warp feeling to me, I would recall at times.

It felt as if things they were saying had to do with the future and things that they shouldn't necessarily know right then, but did. Since I often was aware of strange things, I thought it peculiar that they seemed to be aware of something as well. Yet it felt like they were hiding something.

As they spoke more about what I might want to be when I grew up, they offered me many options to consider. They suggested ideas ranging from, cowboy to doctor, to clown and more. The older man suggested clown, since I wasn't being serious with them and was paying more attention to the store itself rather than them. The owner stated "He already wants to run a store!" and made comments as to if that's what I would keep doing in my future life regardless to what I was supposed to be doing.

They kept inquiring, "What do you want to be when you grow up?" and I finally stopped and looked at them squarely in the faces and said, "Why can't I just be me!" they both laughed and said that you can't do that, you have to be someone. I thought that was a very peculiar thing to say and they went on and asked if I wanted to be a train. I stated back a train? How could a person be a train? And I

> was told "Do you want to be the engine or the caboose or just one of the train cars like everybody else".
>
> I thought they went mad and started to get very confused. They asked the same thing again and I replied "Where is this train going?" They laughed and said, "Does it matter it could just be going in circles." To that I replied, "Well if I am going to be a train why not the caboose!" They laughed and said "Why would you want to be the caboose when the engine is big and strong, gets all the attention and has a bright light in front of it?"
>
> I looked at them and said, "Doesn't a caboose have a light of its own? And if the train is going in circles, then what does it matter if I am pulling everyone else's weight or enjoying the experience?"
>
> **After all I went on -**
>
> "If we are going in circles, I am already in front of the engine, and it is actually trying to get to where I am."
>
> They stood there in disbelief, that such a small child would come back with comments like that. More was said by them that seemed to indicate they knew something more about my future than I was currently offering and they openly wondered how much I knew about it already.

I did not realize at times the things I would say or do would cause me to get attention that I probably shouldn't have received. With this in mind the next memory is disturbing to me in the sense that someone was watching me and having strange influences over me.

> One of my brothers came up to me shortly after the conversation in the store. He had met a man that told him

> to ask me if I wanted to see what I looked like when I became older.
>
> I was confused as to what this meant and part of me was wondering if the man was real or if it was someone my brother had heard in his head.
>
> I said, "Yes, I would like to see myself when I am older." My brother seemed determined that I should. My brother seemed as though he was on a mission as to what he was talking about.
>
> He told me, that the man said that he had to say exactly what he was about to say, in fact he had to even say that. He then went on to say some things that sounded very strange and I really wasn't sure what all the words meant.
>
> He told me I had to repeat the words exactly as he told me. I believe he might as well have said something to the effect that this could never be spoken about again.
>
> The things he was having me say seemed like a very long riddle. It was like he was speaking from memory while in a trance as he spoke.

Though of course back then my childlike consciousness and ego states didn't know what a hypnotic trance actually was.

> At the end of the riddle he said something to the effect of, "Now walk behind the apartment building that we live in and go up to the door to the basement, and put your fist through the window, and you will see what you will look like when you are older."

*I looked at him in a daze, then walked behind the apartment building that we lived in. I went up to the basement door with the window in it, and put my fist through it.*

*As my small fist broke the window, I saw my reflection in the dark glass. It was like I suddenly went into slow motion and all of time stopped.*

*I suddenly wasn't seeing my reflection any more but was seeing a man staring at me. He wasn't behind the door, it was as if I was somewhere else and this man was staring at me with a blank look on his face.*

*He blankly looked at me and then turned and walked away into a crowd of people and disappeared. I noted his hair being slicked back and I really did not like the style of it, as strange as a thought that was to me.*

*I was bothered by what I saw overall and confused why he seemed lost in the crowd as he walked away and wasn't sure what that would mean for my future. I wasn't happy with what I was seeing or who I thought I would turn out to be.*

*When I pulled my fist out of the window, I was in shock. My brother acted surprised that I just did that and possibly he was genuinely shocked and didn't recall what actually transpired between the both of us.*

*He brought me upstairs to my mother to take care of my bleeding hand, and for me to explain why I just broke the window. I was told that I would get in trouble for it from the landlord.*

*No one seemed to believe me when I told them my brother told me to do it. Of course why would they, due to the fact, why would I do what he told me to begin with?*

When I look back at this memory this story holds a huge impact for me. I was hypnotized by a stranger, or someone, or something, through my brother. That itself shows the danger I was in as a child, or was I being given a gift of insight to later use and learn from.

The part of this memory, that is even more peculiar, is when many years later I would go to Florida and visit Disney World. While walking around amongst the crowds, I came across a sign on a building that said look in this window and see your future.

*I walked up the steps, not sure what to expect. I looked and saw my face in the window for it was a dark colored mirror. The people that had just looked in previous to me turned and looked at me and laughed. They knew I had just been duped like them on this practical joke that Disney had created.*

*Of course I had a blank stare on my face. I just realized I had not only seen my face, but as I walked back into the crowd of Disney World feeling lost, I realized I had seen myself from the past, as well. I was within that spot in time, when I had seen into my future as a little kid. I had put my hand through the window which served as a window thru time for me.*

That was the exact moment in time that I had seen into, with my hair slicked back walking seemingly lost into a crowd.

I still have the scars on my left hand from the experience as a child of putting my fist thru that basement window.

*At some point it was decided to move from the apartment which we lived in, that was in the building above the laundry mat in the center of town. We moved to a very old house out on the outskirts of the town surrounded by many fields and a huge apple orchard.*

*In my memories I recall it sounding and feeling like we were moving very far away. I heard thoughts within myself that it might be safer out in the country, away from so many people in the center of town.*

*The house was huge to me the first time in. I was amazed discovering all the rooms. The ceilings seemed very tall. There was a room on the first floor and one right above it on the second floor, that were the largest rooms I had ever seen in a house.*

*The house was run down and needed much work to clean it up. My mother was determined that it could be done and it would be a good move for us. I wanted to move in that day, even though the place was a mess and dirty. I pleaded to be able to help clean the house to move in faster. When we did start working in the house, I remember that I was given a broom and dustpan, and even though I really didn't do much cleaning or be of help, I felt like I did so much.*

*The yard was huge to me. There were three out buildings, one turned out to be a playhouse for us to play in. There was a shed and then another long building that had stalls, to fit automobiles or something. I really wasn't sure what*

> the long building was originally for. The dirt driveway was extended with a half circle of sorts that went from the road to the front of the house and then curved round the outbuildings back to the road.

Life got much more complex within this old house. As an adult I was told that it was the oldest house in that town.

> The things I heard from the spirit realm got louder. It was now becoming much more obvious to me that it didn't seem like everyone had the experiences I was used to having and to what I thought was normal. Before the experiences would slip in and out of my states of consciousness in a way that seemed so natural it didn't leave ripples in the other states of consciousness and I didn't really notice the strangeness of it all.

> I started to realize there where much bigger secrets being hidden by people and there were secret circles of awareness within people. It was all a huge game it seemed and I wanted nothing to do with it.

**The premonitions were getting larger - I started hearing warnings as well.**

> I remember vividly standing in the dirt driveway looking across the street wondering, are the voices I am hearing in my head voices of people hiding behind the old stone walls telepathically sending me messages? Or am I hearing ghosts or are aliens trying to communicate with me? The more I got quiet inside of myself, the more I could understand the words I was hearing and feeling within me. They told me things that would happen to me later in life, they fore warned me of things.

*I remember at around five years of age, pushing my bicycle up a hill near my house. I was behind my brother who was peddling away from me since he was stronger.*

*As I struggled with my bike and being tired I heard loudly a male voice in my head forewarn me that "You need to be very careful of Priests – some will try to marry you and others will try to have sex with you and some may try to kill you."*

*I remember repeating it back to myself several times trying to actually understand what it meant. It really did not make sense to me, why would a priest want to marry me for one?*

*And then I realized it didn't mean he wanted to marry me but rather marry me to someone else. The other two scenarios felt very dark and scary, as if I would sink into a large hole if I considered what it meant. I didn't want to visualize what that meant though some horrible images did flood my mind.*

*Before fully understanding what I had just heard my brother had stopped and asked me what I was doing, since I was just standing there.*

***I yelled back to him in confusion what I just heard.***

*After yelling it a few times, since he either wasn't hearing me or he was mystified as to the combinations of words coming out of my mouth, he came back to me and asked me why I was asking that question and I told him. He told me why those three things might occur and told me to never repeat it again or I may be in danger and he took me home.*

Many years later, it started becoming public knowledge what some priests indeed had done to little children. Hearing about all the sexual abuses to little boys in the past, made this memory flood back to me as to how I was forewarned of it.

I would continue to meet grown men that were abused as children. Each person I met came forward and told me of their abuse and why they did not believe in god. They did not believe there was even such a thing as people having spirits. They further claimed that there was no such a thing as heaven. I realized the gravity of what the men that abused their priesthood had done.

Not only were these children robbed of their childhoods, they were robbed of their awareness of their connection to their spirit and in fact, any awakening knowledge, of what their soul contained within.

**Childhood was a very scary place of not understanding what was going to come after me as I grew up.**

It got much scarier when in living detail I started to see much clearer things that would happen to me later in life.

> *I started to hear within my mind that a man wanted to meet and talk to me. I wasn't sure if I should meet him, or even how I would meet him.*

> *I was just a little kid and I couldn't tell my mother, that I heard in my head, that some man needed to tell me something to protect me. Yet I didn't even know who he was and I really didn't know where I was supposed to meet him.*

> *I didn't know if I should meet him. Or if indeed it was safe in meeting him.*

*All I knew was he wanted to meet me and I felt I had to meet him even after being forewarned what 'men' may try to do to me later in life.*

*I sensed he was trying to offer me something of protection and I didn't seem to have any other man protecting me.*

*After working with what I was hearing for a couple days I sensed I was supposed to go to the center of town to meet him and it was too far for me to walk or ride my bike.*

*As it happened my mother had an upcoming appointment at the hairdressers in town so I planned to meet him then.*

*I hoped this would not be too late of a time to meet, since it felt so urgent and it felt like there were time constraints involved.*

*I talked my mother into letting me go with her and after getting there asked for permission to play on the common, in front of the church, across the street from the building the hairdresser was in.*

*I finally got on the common and knew this was where I had to meet him. I had to find out what the urgent thing was that he needed to tell or show me.*

**I started looking for him.**

*No one else was on the common and I didn't see a man walking towards me. I wondered, do I go in the church and look for him? I wasn't comfortable going into the church alone no matter what type of church it was after what I was told a few weeks back.*

*All this confusion was circling inside my mind and then suddenly I realized I was in the church.*

*It was as if I ran in the church, but I didn't recall going through the doors though suddenly, somehow, I was standing inside the church.*

*I was in what seemed like the basement. It looked like the same area that I once went to kindergarten at within that church. Yet the room seemed different somehow.*

*The man was in long robes in front of me, and started talking to me and gesturing and asking me questions. He seemed like he was above me at the same time as if he was standing on a stage or taller than he should be for where he was standing. I was confused by this, but he stood there, or so I thought, and was determinedly trying to get my attention to focus on what he was saying.*

*He was telling me to pay attention and not look away. As he would do this, he made a strange noise and gestured his hand to the left, which for me was looking to the right. And as I looked in that direction it was as if I was being propelled into the future and seeing what seemed like a future me. Yet the more I traveled into the future image I was seeing, the more I didn't recognize who it was that it appeared I was becoming.*

*I was seeing and feeling things I didn't comprehend with the mind state of the little boy that I was.*

*I didn't like what I was seeing or feeling inside. This whole experience was making me feel like I shouldn't have come and I didn't want to look anymore.*

*He kept telling me to not look away from him yet he would move his arm to make me look over to where he was gesturing and I was getting confused.*

*I didn't understand if I should look at him or where he was gesturing to. What I was seeing and feeling inside, as I looked at either place, seemed too painful to witness.*

*I would look away from the pain of what I was seeing in front of me of who it seemed I would become, and the pain and suffering I would go through. I could not comprehend the suffering and how I could go on and live the life of pain that was being shown to me that lay ahead in my future.*

*This man would demand that I not look away. I just felt more confused as to what he was telling me to do. The things I was seeing and feeling, felt like I was going into a huge black hole of pain.*

*I was a small child and I could not understand how any person could survive the mental and emotional torture that the man I was supposed to become would endure.*

***I did not want to go there.***

*I kept looking away due to the pain I was feeling. He kept making that strange noise demanding me to look again and keep looking and to not look away. According to him I needed to look to the end of what he was showing me. Yet it was so painful to me. I kept looking away crying out I can't go on.*

*I did not think I could comprehend all the levels of consciousness I was experiencing and the pain in the life of the person I was seeing into, which according to this man in front of me was my future life.*

*Each time I was pushed to look deeper and further it felt as if a baseball bat was being slammed into my spine. It felt as if each disc of my spine was hit one at a time. With the strike of each disc, I was slammed into another state of consciousness and dimension of pain and suffering.*

*He was trying to get me to see something, to possibly learn something, yet it seemed too painful for me to experience. If this indeed was my life to come, how could I survive all that and why would I want to go on I wondered.*

*The noise he was making was so strange. It was like he was saying "Who" but it sounded like the noise an owl would make at the same time. I partially thought he was saying "Who are you" or this is "Who you are" but then it had more of an "H" sound to it and that with the hand gestures and everything I was feeling I felt so dizzy and confused.*

*I was dizzy and confused and time was running short he told me.*

*Someone was coming he said and I had to leave. He told me to go and I started to turn yet did not see a door or really know where I was.*

*I was more confused and just wanted to get away from everything I was experiencing there. Yet all I saw was a window and asked "can I go out the window?" to which he laughed and said "Yes!" very loudly, that the window would work as well and that it would be somehow humorous for the future as well as offer me protection now.*

**All of a sudden my mother was standing next to me.**

*My mother was yelling and shaking me, to come to my senses to listen, so she could calm me down since I was not listening.*

*I realized I was still standing outside. I never went into the church. All that time in fact my physical body was running around the big pine tree. I was yelling at the tree the words I was saying to the man offering me the portal to the visions of my future.*

*My mother asked me what was going on stating that the ladies at the hairdressers could hear me screaming from over there. Seeing me run around the tree from their window they thought I must be crazy.*

*I could feel my mother's deep embarrassment from inside of myself.*

*I could feel her love, but also her total confusion, as to what to do with me and what all this looked like to others.*

*I stood there and the memory of what just happened was pushed into my subconscious mind. Another level of a confused ego state replaced the former and I partially forgot again.*

That wouldn't be the last time I would see so starkly into my future. Yet that memory, that experience, would continue to affect my awareness of wondering who was that man and what was his intention and what did I not see that I was supposed to see. It stayed in my subconscious and depending on the triggers of emotions I would be exposed to, it would come flooding back into my conscious mind like a whirlwind.

Many years later I would relate this story to one of my students that I was facilitating the teaching of Reiki to. Often in the style of teaching I offer, I will explain things I have been through. I show my issues and how I have learned to deal with them as an example. For me it is a way to say I am not better than anyone else. I have issues as well. When we come together and open to the space in front of us, that space itself, can teach us as we learn to discern it.

> *As I spoke of the strange "Hooting" noise of the man in the vision and how it would be used while seemingly propelling me into the future my student stopped in shock and stared at me and said, "You really do not realize what you are saying to me?"*
>
> *She went on to explain that she recently had been at one of her therapists offices and saw a poster on the wall. She was compelled to the poster, due to the fact one of the men in the poster she thought was me. She said she stood there confused as to why I would be on this poster in her therapist's office and wondered what the poster was about.*
>
> *Her therapist explained that the poster was for the "HU" which for some is considered the sound of god. She stated that when you use this sound in the appropriate way it can propel you into future awareness. The man that she thought was me on the poster was one of the men from the organization that promoted the use of this technique - this particular path to the awareness of god.*

As happens with the grace of the spirit realm, we often are shown things at the appropriate times to then transfer that knowledge or awareness as if synchronicity to those we are supposed to.

## Fast forward, backwards to some time in my childhood

*I am riding my bicycle, down the big hill, from the apple orchard next to our house. I am going much faster than I can handle on the bike but I am feeling the breeze on my body and am feeling alive and free.*

*A car is driving up the hill and I move to the side of the road to get out of the way. I hit a patch of sand. The bike goes skidding and I fall to the ground with the bike, or so it seems. Then I begin sliding down the hill on my body.*

*How can a person feel so alive and free in the midst of all this?*

*There is much more going on in these moments than the physical realm shows as the spirit realm is preparing to take action even before the car appears.*

## The car stops, yet I slide under it, possibly at the same time –

*I would realize much later that I had sand ground into my hands and some of my face and yet I am oblivious to pain or blood on me.*

*I get up fast from under the car, and the two ladies in the car jump out in terror at the same time that a child may have just died under their car.*

*As they run panic stricken to see if I am alright, I very calmly interrupt them and say I am sorry for scaring them. I offer an apology while asking if they are alright.*

*This of course shocks them even more, but in the opposite direction of where they were headed in their worries about* me. Now they are looking at me as if a miracle was just performed in front of them.

The driver was professing her apologies as if it was her fault I landed under her car.

The other lady was confused. She seemed distracted by feeling the awareness, of a body still under the car. Yet, I seemed to be standing in front of her calmly distracting her from what she was apparently seeing into.

Spirit was busy setting things back into order-

They wanted to take me to get help. I told them I lived at the house right around the corner. I wasn't in pain and would be alright, there was nothing wrong with me.

They asked me and my brother to get in their car so they could drive us up the road to the house but I replied no.

Of course I was told in the past by my parents never to accept rides with strangers and my brother was with me so he could walk home with me.

Spirit was guiding me that I needed to "walk" to reset the senses into the body, to become grounded with the earth again.

The ladies offered to put the bikes in the back of their trunk. So we allowed that and they drove up the road alongside us walking since the house was only a few hundred feet away.

At the house we recovered the bikes, while explaining that our parents were not home at the time. They would be home shortly but I was fine and they could and should go.

> When I finally did go inside I was amazed as I washed up at the blood that was on my face. I was happy again in a way I could not describe, I seemed like a different person.

**The memory that seems to connect to this event in my life happens a short time later within two weeks.**

> I recall hearing from my mother that two ladies wanted to meet me. She told me that I should spend time talking with them. Even though I really did not want to meet them, I was told by my mother it would be polite of me and I should do it.
>
> I believe I was told it was the two ladies from the accident that wanted to see how I was now, and talk to me since they liked me so much.
>
> Though, I recall my brother saying other things to me – he often seemed to like to mess with my head for some reason so I really wasn't sure what to believe at times from what he said to me if it was true or not.
>
> From what I recall my brother said was that the ladies where really from somewhere else and that they wanted to take me away from the family – that is unless I was hearing that from a spirit.
>
> Sometimes as a child becoming aware of things was rather confusing since some things were so much to grasp.
>
> I wasn't sure where the knowledge was really coming from. Maybe it was a spirit speaking through my brother, but there was much confusion for me regarding this brother and the circumstances I found myself in when around him.

> Anyhow, I recall cleaning my room and getting ready for the meeting. Though, what I really did was clean my room to the point of being tired and then shoving everything else into my big closet to make the room look clean.
>
> When I gave the tour of my bedroom I, of course, opened the closet and showed and told them what I did. I explained as I went on how the closet was so large it was like a room itself and how I felt there might be a secret door somewhere in the closet that would lead to another room - but I hadn't found it yet.

Later I did find that secret room in that old house. It was behind the closet. The secret door I found was not in the closet but just outside the bedroom door itself. It was disguised as if it was just a wall covering the chimney. Though, if you moved the little wall, which you could, and entered, you realized there was space on the side of the chimney. If you went around the chimney it led to a little hall and an actual hidden room in the house.

> Of course I wasn't the one that showed me where the door was when I finally listened, it was one of my invisible friends.

**Back to that day with the two ladies**

> As we sat on the floor, of that big bedroom that I shared with my two brothers, the ladies started talking to me. My brother seemed determined to be part of this sharing circle and sat with us while my mother was downstairs in the kitchen.
>
> To this day I am not really sure who the two women were. Are they the ladies from when I fell off my bike and slid under their car? Possibly they came from some social

service organization checking on me since people talked about the fact I was peculiar and possibly there was something wrong with me. My brother did tell me that many people were discussing me. Was it that some thought I was not being taken care of properly and that needed to be looked into?

Was there something else? Could it actually be all the same things including the fact that they were the same two ladies I had met previously? When I was more concerned with their welfare, as opposed to the fact I was actually hurt.

I do not recall much of the beginning of the conversations, it seemed like we talked about my interests and my brother seemed like he wanted more of the attention on him than me.

Then I recall the ladies took out some small items from their pocketbook and laid them out in front of us. There were many items. I was fascinated more with what on earth are these ladies doing with these items and why are they showing them to us to look at, rather than paying a lot of attention to the items in front of me.

My brother seemed to realize more of what was happening than I did regarding their intent, or so it seemed to me.

Most of the items did not really catch my attention, though there were two, maybe three, that seemed to stand out to me for some reason.

I felt held back some, as if I should not show my interest. My brother seemed once again to want to direct what was going on in this little experience and I heard, or maybe sensed something that had me confused.

*I am really not sure if I heard my brother say this in whispers or if it actually came from him. Was a spirit speaking through within me? Or was I hearing a spirit speak through my brother but telepathically and not from his lips.*

**But what I recall I was hearing was not to let them be aware of the item or items I really found interest in.**

*Something strange was happening here on many levels of my awareness. The ladies picked up all the pieces and in a way seemed to notice that even though I outwardly showed interest in one piece that in actuality my interest was in another piece. That piece seemed to hold the most interest to them as if they were waiting to see if that was the piece I would chose.*

*Then something happened that I will never forget. I do not recall what brought it on or how it started, whether it was something being said to me or if I was touched by one of the ladies and that was the start. But, as I sat there I started to have a vision in front of them and they started conversing with me to hear what I was seeing.*

*The visions were some of the most extreme visions I had, that I can recall, up until that point.*

**I started to see into thirty - forty or more years of what appeared to be my life unfolding.**

*I was around five years old or so – and I was seeing that as I grew up people would call me a homosexual. I asked out loud, what is a homosexual and why are people calling me this? Why do they hate me because of it? Why are they telling me I am going to hell, and that I am no good?*

*I was upset, concerned, and even horrified that I would grow up and be hated by people that didn't even know me for things I didn't even comprehend. I saw I would be abandoned, ignored and ostracized before I even had a chance with strangers.*

*When it was explained and I started to realize what sex was I then became confused why anyone would want to have sex with anyone to begin with.*

*I was seeing into what seemed like a very sad life of being judged and not loved by others and a deep sense of being lost and trying to survive.*

*Even though I felt strangely detached from what I was seeing inside of me, it felt like it was such a tragic life that I was seeing unfold in my future and I wondered how and why I would continue on.*

*I saw so much so fast. I witnessed my future-self watching television through these stages that I would later learn would be called ego states of consciousness.*

*I saw future world events unfold during these times of watching news reports on the television, within the vision.*

*I saw a polish pope come to be and how the world was surprised a Polish man would become pope.*

*As I explained this with my little five years old mind and ability of communicating I asked what a Polish "poop" was. As a child I often slurred certain words and this word "pope" was a new one for me.*

*The ladies laughed and explained what a pope was. They asked me if I wanted to be one when I was older since they claimed to know I was baptized Catholic. They stated that it would be wonderful for our country to have an American Pope.*

*I replied that it was this polish man's life-long dream and wish to be a pope and I couldn't take that away from him. I told them how much of a good man he was and that he deserved the position from all the things I could see as I looked into his life and dreams.*

*I saw many more things as the ladies were busy listening and I recall them rustling through their pocketbooks looking for something to write on.*

*They seemed not too surprised by all this, as if they were hoping or waiting for me to somehow magically open up and share all this knowledge. They actually replied to various things I said as if they already knew or were told about certain things I was discussing that would happen in the future.*

**I foresaw two George Bushes as Presidents, and that really threw the ladies for a moment.**

*They seemed to acknowledge they knew about one, but two?*

*There would be two George Bushes as Presidents?*

*I explained that they wouldn't be two Presidents at the same time. One would be the son of the other and many would say he actually stole the election and then call him King George due to his behaviors. To that they were* shocked and asked if the United States was going to become a monarchy in the future. I had to clarify a few things for them to understand what I was seeing in the future.

They asked me if I wanted to be president when I grew up. I recall telling them I wouldn't be allowed to be and they told me that everyone in this country has a chance and a right to become president. They stated if I wanted to be the president I could for I was very special.

They told me that we live in a free country. I stated all that wasn't actually true and in reality I wasn't any more special than anyone else.

I did state that this "King George" would make comments publicly implying to people that understood that he was only the President of "some of the citizens of the country" and they were confused by those comments as well.

The visions continued to unfold very fast. I didn't seem to feel any emotions to the depths as I did in the previous experience with the man at the church when I saw into my future.

This experience was as if I was watching life unfold from the outside as if it was someone else's body I was living in that I really didn't have a connection to other than seeing the pain and loss of suffering. In the other experience I felt like I was actually in my body during each portion of the visions.

I moved through the visions faster and faster. It all sped up and then suddenly it was as if I was flying into the sun. I screamed out about that fact and the lady sitting closest to me moved my head in the opposite direction and said *something out loud like "To the moon and back" or "To the moon with you" or something very strange dealing with the moon.*

**All of a sudden the overwhelming sensation of being lost in the burning sun disappeared.**

*Within my mind I was feeling a sensation that felt much calmer and cooler as if I was sitting there overtaken by the presence of a full moon. I sat there losing myself in the image and feeling as if I was being engulfed by the lunar elements.*

*The lady sitting furthest from me quickly asked the other lady if she had tape or something in her purse. The lady seemed determined that tape was what she needed to fix what was going on - as odd as that sounded to the part of me that was still aware of them.*

*When she couldn't find the tape she pulled out a piece of gum and quickly chewed it. She then stuck it to the middle of my forehead – the spot I would later in life understand as "the mind's eye".*

*At some point towards the end of all this, I recall the ladies asking about where I would be later in my life. They also made comments on where they should be from all the things I had said as to what would be going on in the world in our future.*

*I recall vividly one of the ladies saying that she was planning on doing something at a teaching hospital that would be created in the future somewhere in Worcester or Shrewsbury Massachusetts.*

It seemed odd to me as to where her seemingly previous knowledge must be coming from. She already seemed to have known about this future hospital and I wondered in my head as to what was really going on in this "life" I found myself within.

**I wondered what strangers really know that they are not letting on.**

I don't recall how much time happened after that. But I recall taking the gum off my forehead and saying something like "why did I have gum on my forehead?" and if I recall clearly the lady claimed that I had put it there myself.

My mother who was downstairs seemed to be hearing some of this commotion from the floor grate and yelled up as to what the hell was going on up there? At that point the ladies seemed flustered and my mother started to yell to them to get the hell out of the house. It suddenly seemed like she realized something that she hadn't before.

**Just Because Others Cannot Make Sense of You,**

**Does not mean that You are Senseless.**

Later in life when I took a class in clinical hypnotherapy I was able to better understand all these states of consciousness I was seeing into.

The reason I took this class was to get a clearer understanding on consciousness. I wanted to understand what the states of consciousness were. I was determined to learn how to not be hypnotized and telepathically controlled by others.

It was obvious that people needed to learn this to regain their empowerment from those things that had control of them.

One of the first things I learned in this class was that hypnosis is naturally occurring all the time. Our states of consciousness are effected by people places and things around us – that we drift up or down into various states of consciousness all the time.

It's commonly said that we only use 10% of our minds. That is what people call our conscious mind. Our subconscious mind is the other 90% of our mind. The more that we are able to delve into the subconscious mind the more we are able to access and open up more levels of consciousness for ourselves.

It seems to me that in the western world we are trained in school to squeeze our synapsis, our brain cells to think. Though in fact, everything that we read or see, hear and sense is actually recorded within the many levels of our minds.

The issue at hand is how we bring forth the required information when it is needed.

Reading and rereading our class subjects and material over and over again may be putting the information in files all over our mind, cluttering up every file cabinet we have within us. We assume it is easier to access when needed, but what is that really doing to us?

The more that we center and balance our emotions and energies when we study, the more that balanced energy itself gets stored with the information we are assimilating into our consciousness. The more we do this the more we are able to retrieve information easily.

**The consciousness becomes stable and clear with an ability of great depths.**

Within my memories, of what the average person may call supernatural or psychic experiences, are stored my reactions and the reactions of others around me that occurred during those events from those experiences. Often those reactions of mine or the reactions of the other people are what has made it so I can remember more easily things that have happened that have shifted my states of consciousness from one level to another so dramatically at times.

It is as if keys or breadcrumbs on the past, so to speak, have been left within my memories to show me the truth of these experiences when I look back at them.

Our subconscious mind holds onto and represses memories and experiences that we are not able to deal with in order to protect us. It keeps these experiences from coming back and re-harming us in our minds. It does this by creating a new state of ego within our consciousness. The former state of consciousness goes to the back and a new state of consciousness comes forward and blocks out the issues we are not able to deal with.

As we grow into adulthood and beyond we may have many traumatic experiences that the mind continually creates a series of ego states to manage and recover from.

The subconscious mind is very busy doing many other things as well, it works to regulate our blood flow and heal cuts and wounds. The subconscious mind balances all the intricate happenings within our bodies including the growth and maintenance of our cells all while blocking and holding onto things we cannot deal with.

The more we work to live a balanced life, think and live within a holistic model of mind/body and spirit balance the more our subconscious mind is helped in its processes.

Possibly one of my favorite phrases the last few years of my life as an empathic therapist is to "Work with our processes".

We can work through our issues and learn not to be reactive and instead to see/witness what goes on around us without getting lost in the mix of reactions. Being active when needed and proactive when possible is important. Then we are able to take charge of our lives.

The more we are able to let go and BE then the more we are able to exist within our higher consciousness and bring forth light into our lives as opposed to confusion and darkness.

An amazing thing happens within our bodies and subconscious when we "work with our processes". If we allow ourselves the space to be and grow and overcome our issues from the past, the more our subconscious is able to let go of all those things it suppresses to protect us from.

When we learn from these experiences there is more energy and attention available for the subconscious mind to give all the other intricate functions it serves. It releases its hold on the various states of ego it used to have to protect us from. The subconscious mind then has more stability to take care of our health.

We need to integrate all our levels of consciousness. If we allow the little boys and little girls within us to grow up, to possibly see things more clearly, to understand life for what it is without judgments of ourselves or others, the more we let light into our circumstances the more we can connect to our higher self.

When we connect to our higher self the more that connection strengthens to the higher realms of life and we see positive results from such endeavors.

From my experience I would say the more we do this, we are able to come to our senses and balance the energies of our spirit to bring forth the true connection to our soul and all there is.

Before I go further on thoughts and concepts of consciousness and indeed the prospect that humanity is actually currently overcoming a hypnotized spell of consciousness and telepathic control, let's soon go back to my childhood.

There are more things, than there is space, within this book to tell and explain that I experienced within my childhood. In another book I may go into other areas of these things, though as well I am trying to be careful here as to not tell stories that would cause too much confusion for the person reading this and their current state of consciousness.

One of the things I have learned is that as a person develops the ability to let go of beliefs that no longer serve them, they need to have stronger beliefs to replace the others they are letting dissolve away.

**Think of yourself as a house or a temple for a moment.**

If we suddenly realize that the foundation holding this vessel up, the structures of consciousness that make up our beliefs are based on things we learn are not true or real then we need to either have a very solid foundation of faith or learn to start co-creating the ability to be conscious faster than the former structures of consciousness start dissolving.

Within my various states of consciousness growing up were many levels of fear.

Neal Donald Walsch has said: "Fear is an acronym in the English language for "False Evidence Appearing Real".

**False**

**Evidence**

**Appearing**

**Real**

**FEAR = False Evidence Appearing Real**

I was trying to be a child yet at the same time in a multidimensional way I was dealing with the processing of what I had seen that looked like it may be the rest of my life. I then had to come to terms with then living that life when I already had seen and felt how much pain was actually going to be coming at me.

One of the things I was blocking within that midst of fear was that I also was seeing into what may have been some of my past lives. I saw into lives that did not seem like just any lives. The enormity of what I saw was beyond the mind of a five year old.

The more I reacted and was not present, the more life seemed to happen at or to me. I had to learn to realize that life is a co-creation it does not happen at or to us.

**I often say: "Boredom is a lack of empowerment".**

There were many times in childhood I felt very alone. I would lose myself in play or get lost in the reaction of a toy or something I had wanted to have so I could blur out my awareness of things around me and what I had foreseen in growing up.

I didn't see a way out of the impending darkness coming at me.

At night I would wake up having night terrors of seeing and feeling people at war. I would fall asleep into dreams of death and destruction of seeing and feeling overcome by things that seemed to becoming from the history of the planet itself.

I would wake up screaming many nights and not be able to sleep.

> *One night, a spirit came and showed me mentally how to move the energy of my mind so that I could turn off the things I was sensing. I could allow space for myself to be, so that I could fall asleep.*
>
> **I was told that I would need to wait till I was older, until it was much safer for me to come forward.**
>
> *I was told that at my young age with no one physically around to protect me I was in danger if others knew of my awareness - I needed to wait until a time when many others would surround me with their own awareness and I wouldn't stand out in danger.*
>
> *I needed to wait until a time that humanity itself was ready to deal with its ascension.*

As a child, spirit was teaching me something I would later learn in life when I would study an energetic therapy called Reiki. I was taught how to mentally move the energy of my mind to protect myself in creating a boundary of what I was seeing and sensing.

That exact energetic technique was one of the first tools to learn many years later within the facilitation of my Reiki training. When I look back at this realization I am not sure when the facilitation of my Reiki training actually started due to this.

As I was growing up I was able to look back to these memories, when I was not lost in a reactionary realm of pain. I would wonder about that night and what spirit spoke to me about. I wasn't sure who that spirit really was, or at least I didn't recall if I did know and that was a concern to me.

What if I wasn't supposed to listen to that spirit? What if I was to overcome my issues all on my own? Was that five year old supposed to understand all that was happening and take control of his life on his own?

**I was in a child's body – but my awareness was not of just a child.**

I was learning to work with the faculties of being a child but as well integrating the multidimensional awareness of future and past time - space continuum and bring forth the alchemies of being.

> **If Fear is: False Evidence Appearing Real**
>
> **Then FAITH is:**
>
> **Fears**
>
> **Ascending**
>
> **Intuitively**
>
> **Towards**
>
> **Heaven**
>
> **FAITH = Fears Ascending Intuitively Towards Heaven**
>
> False evidence appearing real ascending intuitively towards heaven becomes FAITH.

### *Stop calling me Kevin!*

*There was a day somewhere back in those times that I sat and pondered why everyone called me Kevin.*

*My name was Keith, not Kevin and I was really tired of people calling me Kevin. Of course the name Kevin was more popular than Keith. People didn't recall my name due to that fact it was more unusual, so often they called me Kevin.*

*I sat and pondered, fed up with all the things I seemed to deal with. I was tired of the pain I felt and how I never seemed to fit in anywhere in life. Often people didn't even call me my real name.*

*I sat and thought. I do not want to be called Kevin. I do not want to be called Kevin. I ran this statement through my head so many times it spun through my mind until I said defiantly, "I do not want to be called - Kevin anymore!"*

*And then suddenly I flashed on to the reality from where I do not know it came - but I suddenly knew that when I grew up one of my best friends, who would protect me from others, would be Kevin Moore!*

Later in my life I would meet a friend by the name of Kevin Moore that has protected me in the ways he has been able and there is a story in that itself which I will discuss more of later.

As I look back on that memory, I assume part of the reason I was able to pull out that realization was that I had seen it previously in other visions of my future. I had repressed it into other states of ego.

I realized as a child, there were times I could speak in rhymes somewhat like a riddle mixing words together and I would become aware of things. It was a very strange thing when it happened.

One night a relative came over to tell my parents that he got his girlfriend pregnant and the discussion ensued that he would have to marry her.

I sat on the floor listening as my mother spoke with this girl and my step father spoke with the guy in another room.

I listened intently to her name, first and last and the realization that she would now receive the last name of the guy.

Her full name ran through my mind and her new name ran through with it. As the two names became intertwined into one I became aware of another girl who had parents that I sensed would pass away from a plane crash. Her name being the same first name as this girl in front of me, and later in life would marry someone that had the same last name as the girl in front of me currently had.

**The riddle, the rhyme was alive in me spinning out facts of awareness from the future.**

I thought out loud how sad it was that the parents of this girl would die in a plane crash. I mentioned I would know her someday when I owned a flower shop and she would be one of my best customers.

My outburst caused pandemonium in the room. The girl presently in front of me was rightfully confused by what I was saying.

*My mother told me to be quiet and stop speaking, though I recall saying more. I was tired of being shut up, of being shut off, I was tired of feeling held back, tired of feeling so alone.*

***I spoke about more of the future and of my concerns that I could see from there.***

*I made comments about things that would happen to me.*

*I made comments about things that would happen to our family.*

*I made comments that someday it wouldn't matter because I wouldn't be here since I would become someone else. It wouldn't matter to my mother because even though she would be here, she would not be truly conscious that she actually was.*

*I even made a comment about the future death of a relative.*

*The girl sat in the corner and cried, confused as to what she was just involved in. Somewhere in the incident the girl in fear reacted and called me a devil. That was the boiling point for me to speak further of the future. I shouted in my own anger and confusion that "no I am not the devil, but someday people may call me the antichrist, due to the fact they do not comprehend."*

*I stated that, "They will want and even demand that I perform miracles to show them what I can do. They want to create devils that they can have control over, since they have no control themselves."*

> *I went further and shouted, "They will judge me for the things they make me do and then push me into hell by their own lack of understanding and fears."*

Part of what I admitted to myself, in that outburst, was the fact I was aware, in my future I would be told of my past lives by spirit and my own visions of them.

The lives I would be told and see into, as to who I was would be so large to me that I would have difficulty dealing with the reality of it. I would fear that it was a lie that someone or something was trying to control me with in my future by creating a massive ego trip for me to fall prey to.

I was a child trying to overcome not only my future life but what may have been my past lives all at the same time as trying to actually grow up within the life I was living.

The incident with the two ladies of the vision "to the sun and to the moon and back" that I spoke of earlier had repercussions that would follow me through my life.

I do not know this for fact, but from what spirit has told me and from the experiences I had afterwards - My brother went to school and discussed what happened that day. I was told he was proud that his family was to be part of a huge prophecy, that it was as if his brother was going to be a messiah.

Of course most people that heard the story laughed and thought he was crazy and didn't believe or comprehend the truths of the story. Yet, some actually heard what was said.

As I said earlier I cannot confirm these statements with my own memory of seeing this. It is what I sensed I was told by a spirit and there are many things that happened after that seems to fit this puzzle piece.

My brother started to get advice and instruction from someone. He actively started telling me things to prepare me for my future from what these people where telling him.

If anything the things he told me just confused me and made me more scared. I would be seemingly happily lost in the ego state of a child and then he would throw this information at me. I sensed he thought he was doing right and was only trying to help. Though, I sensed he was getting deeper and deeper into something that didn't feel right to me.

> *One morning my pet rabbit in the hutch outside died. I was told to not go near the hutch, for my own sake, so I did not see what happened and be disturbed.*

*I was told that an animal must have gotten to the rabbit. I overheard my brother make comments that it didn't make sense due to the fact the wire was cut on the cage and that an animal wouldn't cut the wire to get to the rabbit.*

*I remember hearing as well, and I may be remembering wrong since this is such a huge thing to say, but for some reason I recall hearing that there was a small metal crucifix left and that of course no animal wears a cross was stated.*

*As the conversation winded down I heard comments regarding "it must have something to do with that army guy that has been hanging around stalking him".*

I can remember vividly all the way into my 20's there were times people would walk by me on the street and very quietly say things like, "Don't tell you're not safe, they will come and get you."

I have memories of odd things happening around me that most would feel the need to assume I was crazy or becoming crazy because of the fact they themselves were not able to comprehend them.

**Orchard Road, Massachusetts**

If a person cannot comprehend something, that seems so out there, then the easiest thing for them to make sure their belief structure is intact and is strong is to deflect the lack of making sense onto the other person.

> *There was a morning back then that I heard spirit tell me to go outside because I needed to know something. I walked out into the dirt driveway asking within my mind, "What is it I need to know?" I walked over to the old birdbath with the circle of Siberian iris in bloom around it and asked again – "What do I need to know, and where are you and who are you and why are you talking to me?"*
>
> *I heard, "You need to take things slower when you ask questions but first it's important for you to know that later this afternoon you need to go into the old barn and climb up into the rafter and sit and wait."*
>
> *As I was hearing this I was guided to the area the spirit was telling me that I needed to go. I was astounded as to what the spirit was telling me to do and I replied, "I am just a little boy, I am not strong enough to climb up there all alone – I know my brother does but I am not that strong."*
>
> *This spirit told me the exact time for later that afternoon that I had to climb up there and told me I had to do it, that my future depended on it.*
>
> *As the day progressed I was anxiously awaiting the time I was told I would need to climb into the loft and then wait some more and see what would transpire that was so important for my life.*

When the time did arrive I went to the barn and looked up at the rafters and the little loft in the corner. I wasn't sure how I could make it up there. But, I knew my brothers did and I recalled what they would grab onto as they made their way up into the rafters to the loft and I started climbing.

It was so hard for me to climb up to that height, to pull all of my weight up as I went. I struggled with the task that I was told was so important. As I moved I realized that if I used the motion of my movements, each grasp got easier to lift myself and I realized I was in the loft much faster than I thought I would ever have been able to do.

I actually found myself now in the loft waiting, waiting for something, not sure of what I was expecting to happen.

A few minutes later one of my brothers walked into the barn. Then from the other end of the barn a man walked in. I was shocked, suddenly realizing that this was real, something actually was going to happen and I was supposed to watch it happen in front of me.

I noticed with the man was another boy and a girl. I recognized the other kids as ones that my brother sometimes hung out with.

Then a lady started to walk in and stood at the opening of the door. I could tell that the lady was reluctant, I don't think I knew what that word meant back then but I could tell she was really not sure and not ready if she should come in and be part of whatever was going on.

*I was lying in the loft trying to be as quiet as I could. I remember thinking that I needed to even breathe quietly, don't let them hear me breathe I thought. I was in such a heightened state of a mixture of surprise and anticipation tinged with fear.*

***I thought to myself that I shouldn't look too directly at them for they may actually feel me looking if I do.***

*The man was positioning himself as to where he should stand, and where everyone else should be for what he was planning. He had his son stand next to him and his daughter in front. He was demanding his wife come over. He stated that she needed to be part of this for they needed her feminine energy to balance out what they were doing, though she still resisted.*

*Parts of this memory are blurry due to the fact I was trying not to look too hard so I wouldn't be noticed by the intent of my stare. I was starting to get more concerned for what was going to happen. It seemed very strange and the energy of the woman resisting was also making me nervous inside. It was as if I literally could feel her nervousness inside of me.*

*The husband was trying to get her involved in the process, telling her how important that it was. I heard him say what sounded like that they were going to be a part of history. It sounded like he said, "they could be part of his first book and how much of a great honor that would be for their family."*

*If I recall right the man had my brother in front of him and then his daughter in front of his son. I recall hearing that it was less weird if my brother was in front of him, rather than his daughter, yet somehow, it wouldn't be so bad if the daughter was in front of the son.*

*Then my brother got on his knees in front of the man as did the daughter in front of the son. I honestly cannot recall if they were assuming a position as if they were praying on their knees. Or did the father and son have their pants unzipped and it looked like something else?*

*At this point my head seemed like it was spinning. I really wasn't sure what I was witnessing or what was going to happen next. All the energies I was feeling inside and outside of my body had me confused.*

*The mother was still at the door on the other side of the barn not sure what to do. The father was directing the scene below me. It seemed to me, that he was trying to build some sort of energy up them. I was trying to comprehend what I was seeing and hearing. It seemed as if he was expecting something to happen if the two on their knees were able to do something properly.*

*The man was complaining the energy wasn't strong enough. They didn't have much time left if they were going to complete their goal. If I recall correctly his wife mentioned something about needing more love for the energy.*

*After more pleas from the husband, the wife finally came over admitting her concern for what it might "look like" that they were doing, and she was disturbed by that.*

*The wife kneeled before the husband with my brother, and helped with whatever was actually taking place.*

*The husband exclaimed that time was short and it was important for this to take place. Shortly after that the husband started to get excited and said that it was starting to work. It was starting to happen.*

*He was looking in the air towards the middle of the barn near the barn stall openings. I could feel the energy in the barn start to shift. It was if something was starting to form in the middle of the air.*

*The man was getting more and more excited and it seemed an image was starting to form in the middle of the air. The energy was shifting in a very strange way as if something was going to appear right in front of us.*

*It felt as if the image would get stronger and become more apparent the more I allowed it to come in, as if somehow I myself held a key to allowing this image to form.*

*The energy of the image coming through felt as if it was going to be female. The energy that was coming forth into our reality started to actually appear as the spirit of a woman.*

**My head and body were spinning with so many emotions and feelings, I didn't know what to do or think or even feel.**

*I didn't know if this was a good thing or a bad thing. I didn't know if I should be looking or if I shouldn't be looking. Part of me felt like I was in great danger with these people. At the same time I seemed to be hearing a message from this female spirit that seemed to be directed directly at me.*

*The message seemed multidimensional and even coded in a way that I didn't comprehend. Later in life I ran the memories through my mind and feelings. I would realize it seemed to have a time code to it that would make more sense to me as grew older.*

*Within the messages, within the images there seemed to be the spirits of two women. The final image I saw that materialized in front of us was a woman I would personally meet many years later and she introduced herself to me in the thin air of that barn.*

*The first spirit appeared as if it was Mary mother of Jesus. She seemed as if there was a warning that came with her that it was not the time for what was happening to transpire in that way.*

*It got to a state that was more than I could take or feel or experience. I just screamed out loud to the woman I would later meet in my life to not leave me there alone.*

*The image disappeared, I was exposed, and everyone looked at me.*

*I heard a commotion of words from the others. I believe I even heard the man explain something about, "He was here all along!" If he was referring to me I do not know. I do not really even know if those were the exact words I heard in all the confusion.*

*It seemed as if multiple realities could be taking place all at the same time and it just depended on your frame of reference or attitude as to what you would think happened.*

*During this commotion the man's son bolted to the side of the barn I was at. He climbed up into the rafters to me so fast I couldn't believe the speed it seemed. I was terrified, I didn't know if he was coming to beat me up or kill me. He got up in the loft with me and jumped on me. Feelings of terror filled through me. He was much bigger and on top of me. What could I do?*

*I was totally confused because I then realized he was kissing me. He was telling me he loved me and that when I grew up in the future other men would love and kiss me too. He said it would be alright, but he wanted to be the first to kiss me.*

*He told me he wasn't the right one for me. He was going to be "straight" in this life, but that was fine as well.*

*I was trying to get him off me, confused and getting tickled and kissed all at the same time. I was just told and felt I was intimately loved by someone who was leaving me at the same time. I felt violated and messed with emotionally.*

*Later in life these memories came back to me at times. I felt not only violated emotionally but psychologically and spiritually as well.*

**I would also think how could this be real?**

*It is too strange to be true, people would think I was crazy if I told them about this, it must not be real. Maybe I misunderstood what I saw. Maybe I didn't see this. Possibly it was just a dream. I thought, maybe I am crazy and then I would push it back into my subconscious and move onto another state of ego.*

With what I know now in life, if I actually do know any more than I did before I started, I am able to look back at many of the experiences I have had with a wider reference point.

I have learned to react much less than I used to. Not much of anything scares me anymore. I realize fear is a mind killer, that it puts our consciousness on pause as we gasp within and stop breathing.

**When a person reacts in shock to something the reaction is normally a response to take a breath in and then actually stop breathing for a moment.**

The more shock and the more experiences of shock, create layers of spaces within us of not breathing. These layers actually hold blockages of our consciousness and if we choose to "work with our process" we need to allow these layers to dissolve and breathe life back into them.

Homework at the kitchen table

## Colorado

*Leaving the big old house with the apple orchard next door and everything that had happened to me so far in my life, seemed like a mixture of sadness yet relief.*

**It felt like we were moving to another country, it seemed so far away.**

*I knew now that it wasn't over the ocean, my sister and I had that discussion already. It was far away but still in this country. I learned a little about what a country was and that people would still be speaking the same language as us though they may speak it in a funny way.*

*It was going to be a new start in life for all of us, though strangely not all of us were going to go.*

*I was hearing whispers in the family as to some of us may go and others will have to stay behind. In the end it was only me, my older sister, little sister, and my mother and step father that moved to Colorado.*

*I lost my brother that protected me, the one I always felt loved me as his little brother and family even though he was only my step brother.*

*Though I never really told him everything going on in my mind or that I was seeing, I always felt safer when he was around. He was not allowed to go with us and instead moved in with one of his older sisters.*

*My brother that I always seemed to be confused by, that seemed at times to be looking out for my future yet seemed to be treating me harshly in my current reality also would not go with us. That brother would move in with my real father and my oldest brother Danny, the one that had the wild red hair, the one that I barely knew. Life was going to be very different.*

*I also lost the future that I was trying to manifest, my girlfriend, the one I had thought I would grow up and marry and have children with. The one that would play the song "Billy don't be a hero" over and over again for me on her little record player, singing it out loud and telling me I had to listen that it was very important for me and her.*

*It became obvious that the move would mean that my girlfriend and I would become separated. We spoke about writing. We spoke about saving up allowance money to take trips out see each other, though I knew that it was the end of our times together.*

*The things that I had heard from the many voices whispering about me and her in my head were changing.*

*Those voices claiming to know what should have been were losing their say. I often heard voices speaking of that eventful first day that we drove by her parent's house. My mother's old car "the thunderbird" broke down, right at their doorstep. That was how we met.*

Many years later I would bring my shamanic friend John Livingston on a tour of the neighborhoods of my childhood. John has ability of listening to spirit and knowing about geology and ley lines. He would tell me that there was indeed a ley line that cut right through the road on the exact spot the car died so many years ago.

On that tour of The Brookfield's and surrounding towns John would add up and clear all the dark portals. The demons and ghosts attached to those places were removed. He quietly told me what in fact was in those houses I had spent time at. I became aware of what I was really dealing with all those many years ago.

*That was the day I met her. That was the day the voices thought was not chance but rather my destiny, not the other path that some said was coming. With her blonde hair and my dark brown we were called, "Salt and Pepper".*

A strange thing that I have experienced often in my life is that among the many voices in my head I have discovered there are some voices that just seem to not fit in an easy category to understand.

I have had to learn to discern who these voices are. In doing so I have realized they do not seem to fit into the structure of the frame of time I am currently in when I hear them. It's as if someone from another time is watching me and I am hearing or sensing their reactions to what they are seeing as they eves drop on my life.

Over time I have gotten very good at discerning and learning the difference between Ego, Judgment, Personality, Opinion, and even Learned Knowledge. I am aware of things that stand out that relate to these things.

Those five things that I discern are actually part of the main aspect of my facilitation of teaching Reiki and awareness to my current students.

**(Reiki will be more explained for those unaware of it in the chapter "REIKI IS LOVE" further in the book)**

I feel the more that you can discern those five things the easier it is for a person to actually allow the Reiki energy to give them back their free will. It allows the love that Reiki is to flow through them.

The more a person can do this the more they are in fact learning to hold actual space of being not only for them but for another.

With this being said, it becomes much easier to understand what you are sensing around you. You learn to discern your energy from the energy of another person. The more you work at learning to discern your energy fields the more naturally you comprehend and feel what other peoples energies are doing to yours. Or correctly stated: You learn to understand more as to what you are allowing other peoples energies to do to your energies.

**After all another of my favorite phrases goes "life does not happen at us or to us, we co-create with life whether we realize it or not".**

If you have kept up on the research going on in the world of science you would be familiar with the following thought construct. It has been scientifically proven that when a test is being created the scientists have to make it a "blind study" to make sure that the test results themselves are not becoming interfered with by the observation of those same scientists watching the test.

**To put it more plainly the scientists themselves have learned by watching the findings of their tests they are actually affecting the tests by the energy of their observation.**

As I have learned to discern and separate the voices I hear within me, I have learned which are actually within me, as in being my own states of consciousness. I have learned to understand those which are voices that I would expect to hear from people that are not actually voices and in fact are only the recognition of learned expectations of thoughts of other people.

I also have learned to discern voices of disembodied spirits. I have a good recognition of who they are attached to or if indeed they are only the energetic imprint of who the person was, but is actually not even spiritually present.

There are various levels of energies when it comes to disembodied spirits and the energetic awareness and discernment of Ego, Judgment, Personality, Opinion, and Learned Knowledge of those spirits is considered key in understanding what dimension they are from.

I have become aware of what I would call Higher Beings as well as Lower Beings in these realms. It may be more appropriate to refer to these as beings of more light or less light so as to not get lost in concepts of judgment regarding them.

Yes, I have become aware of what would be called demons on others as well as things you could refer to as energetic attachments onto living people. These things can block the spirit and free will of a person from coming through and being clearly connected to their soul.

In all of this discerning, there is something else that just does not seem to fit into this.

It feels as if there is a time warp of sorts. All of a sudden I become aware as if I am being watched. Someone is intently paying attention to me and in doing so they react off of what I am doing. I literally hear in my mind their thoughts, their energetic reactions, sometimes it's as if they are commenting to another that is watching as well.

The part that is telling is the energy I can sense that surrounds them comes through as if from another energetic space of time.

If you have ever suddenly remembered a dream you had months or years previous, as the dream floats back into your consciousness you can often recall what was going on in your life during that time period.

Possibly you remember the dream and you also remember what you did the night before or the morning after awakening from that dream.

It's as if the space of time that the dream was in came forward with your recollection of the dream. That is possibly the closest way that I can describe these experiences.

**The trip to Colorado was in the middle of winter snow storm.**

> It didn't start out snowing, but by time we were in the middle of the trip, so far away from home, sleeping in the back of an old station wagon we were in a blizzard.

*My step father met a trucker at one of the rest stops we stopped at for gas. I can recall the look of shock and sadness on the man's face when he realized there was a family in a station wagon driving cross country in the middle of that blizzard.*

*I remember hearing him say, "You can't continue driving it's not safe to travel!" and my step father saying that, "We have to continue, it would be alright, and we couldn't stop now".*

*I remember the man instructing my step father to follow him. He said he would use his tractor trailer to cut a path through the storm to protect us.*

*I can vividly remember empathically feeling as if I was inside that man.*

*The strength he had, the knowledge that he needed to protect us, and the humble pride he had in doing so, I wanted to feel like that man when I grew up.*

*Colorado was a strange place for me; it was like someone took all the trees away from us. I was used to living in a small town in Massachusetts with trees all around and I didn't realize that it could be different.*

*The mountains were amazing. I realized those things back home that we called mountains were nothing like these, they definitely were only hills, these were mountains.*

*When we got to our destination we stayed with friends of my parents while my stepfather looked for a job and he and my mother looked for a house.*

Christmas came and it was the first time that Christmas did not feel like what I was used to. We were in someone else's house and it was someone else's Christmas tree. Personally I was offended by the whole experience.

There was something about these people I did not like nor did I trust. Of course they were just different people; I was not accustomed to them. "People are people," and everyone has their own quirks. But I was still not impressed by them as a child.

The Christmas present I received from my parents was a blue plastic typewriter. It actually was a left handed typewriter of all things, since I was left handed. I remember being excited I could now start writing a book!

On opening the typewriter and putting paper in it I realized there was something very strange about this typewriter, it was the fact it typed backwards!

We were mystified and tried to see if I was doing something wrong when I typed. Regardless of what we did, it still typed backwards.

I remember going with my stepfather to Sears and returning the typewriter at the sales desk. We tried explaining what was wrong with it. I declared I wanted to keep it, if it could be fixed.

The sales guy admitted he had never heard of a left handed typewriter before. He stated that it must be typing backwards because of the left handed typing. We tried to explain that it was the words themselves coming out backwards, not that it was typing right to left. The words were coming out backwards as if by magic.

*After the sales guy tried typing a few words he was more than mystified. He seemed somewhat freaked out over the whole ordeal. The little boy with the left handed blue plastic typewriter wasn't making him feel all that sure of what was going on with the things coming out of his mouth either.*

*To settle the situation since it couldn't be figured out and there were no replacements for this typewriter, my step father returned it for money and we discussed we would get something else. I can't even recall what I did get instead, but I knew it just wasn't the time to write the book and it would have to wait.*

*I couldn't wait till my parents found a new house. I did not want to continue living with those strangers.*

*On Sundays we kids had a choice of either going to a big church in town that was frightening or we had to stay home and clean up the dog feces in the yard from their pet.*

*Those were was the two options. The one day I stayed home I realized neither option was a good option. The yard looked like no one ever had picked up after the dogs before. The Reverend at the church yelled so loud during his sermons it was scary. He was so angry and clearly full of hatred. It was so painful inside of my body to sit there and hear and feel his tyranny pour off him.*

*I couldn't take it any more - my parents hadn't found a house yet and living where we did was intolerable for me.*

*The lady would go on about going to church yet she swore often. I was amazed that she would buy these magazines in the grocery store called "Playboy" and how she would flaunt it to my mother saying, "I bet you didn't have these* back in Massachusetts at your grocery stores." My mother stood there horrified as she waved it. I noticed that even the sales lady was a bit horrified by this woman's boldness of what "she" called women's liberation.

**The boiling point was during an evening meal of liver.**

We all sat around their table that night and I was told that I had to eat what was served to me. They were not operating a restaurant. They didn't know what was normally done where I was from, but the man of the house told me that I was in his house.

It seemed to me that he definitely wanted everyone to know he was the man of his house.

I stated that I didn't think I could eat the liver and that the smell of it, just in the kitchen, was making me feel sick. I was told I would eat it and all of it and not say a word.

The man of the house brought the plate of liver over to me that he himself prepared. He commented that he gave me an extra big piece to make a man out of me.

I was very quiet realizing that my parents were not going to step in and say anything. My mother I could tell hated being there and my step father did not know what to do about the whole predicament.

In the opinion of the little boy of who I was, I felt this man of the house, was no man and rather just a tyrant. Yet there was no other actual man present to stand up for me or my family.

**I sat quietly and tried to eat the liver.**

*I was literally gagging and trying to force it down. The man of the house told me that pretending to get sick was not helping my cause. I needed to be a man and eat the liver, and all of it.*

*I explained I was not pretending and I did feel like I may be sick and throw up. To which I was told by the man of the house that if I got sick I would have to clean that up myself as well.*

*I tried to swallow. I was thinking I should just allow myself to throw up and be done with it and then I had an epiphany.*

*My mother used to call me her little man and obviously my step father was not going to be a man and protect us so I would.*

*I put my fork down. I spit out the liver I was gagging on and stated very calmly that I was not going to put up with this anymore, that I would not be treated this way.*

*My mother looked at me with surprise, my step father was not sure what to do and the man of the house stated that I had to do what he said since I was in his house.*

*My reply was very calm and to the point explaining that I would not allow myself or my family to be continually treated in this manner and that I was more of a man than he was and I was only a small boy.*

*I stated that if my stepfather was not able to step in and be a man then I would. I went on that even though we didn't have a place to go - we were going to leave because no place was better than this place.*

**Everything in that house ground to a halt at my speech.**

I gave the biggest little speech of my life and was determined if I had to, I would shock them all into change; and to that end within minutes we were out on the street piling into the car.

My stepfather was presumably in the house dealing with the fallout, while trying to get out safely. My mother was shortly behind us kids laughing that she did not know or comprehend what just happened but she was glad it did.

It felt like heaven in that motel room that the five of us shared. My parents organized borrowing money from a relative to find us a new place to live.

My parents bought a mobile home and I was surprised with how nice it looked. I still was not actually happy, deep down inside I felt all alone with no one to turn to. I didn't seem to fit in at school, the other kids said my "Massachusetts accent" as they called it made me speak oddly, and I thought they spoke pretty strange to me.

A couple of the boys picked on me, but the boy that all the girls seemed to dream about, wanted to be my friend. He would come to my house before school so he could walk to school with me.

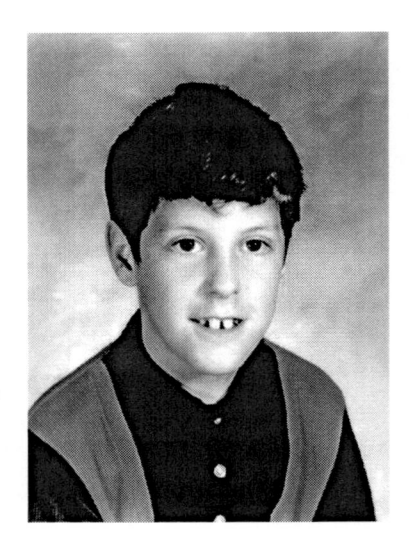

*His house was in the opposite direction closer to the school. It seemed like a good long walk for him every day from what I recall. There was a big trench we would sometimes walk through on the way to school.*

*I liked my new friend a lot. Finally it was like I had someone I might be able to open up to and share what was really going on inside of me.*

*Then that girl appeared - the one that had the name which was the same as a song that I thought was strange.*

*I thought the song was dumb, and really not something as kids we should be listening to. She liked the fact that her name was the same as a song and for some reason it seemed she felt she needed to live up to the theme of the song.*

*So, the "song girl" lived in the same mobile home park as we did. She seemed to be around a lot. In fact, since my friend would walk with me home she now made it seem like he was walking her home instead and it really didn't feel like there was much I could do about it.*

*This was cutting into my time of sharing and bonding and I wasn't pleased about it.*

*"Song Girl" seemed to be in competition with me for the attention of my friend and it seemed in ways she was putting me down.*

*It got to the point, as strange as it was to me - she wanted to learn how to kiss. She claimed we were old enough now and my friend and I would have to kiss her.*

I sensed it went straight to my friend's sense of masculinity and even though he didn't seem really interested in her he would attempt kissing her.

She would berate us in teasing ways to get what she wanted. He would kiss her a little to get her to stop. I tried, but frankly my personal opinion was that I thought she was a sleazy little girl and really not all that pretty.

My friend's attitude was, well she's someone to learn how to kiss with for the future, and he actually said something along those lines to me.

When we both were attempting to kiss her at the same time there where a few moments it felt like he wanted to kiss me also, or maybe it was instead. As much as I wanted to only spend time with him I was disturbed by this girl and her actions.

**My aunt and uncle and one of my cousins were going to be moving to Colorado with us soon.**

They were going to buy a mobile home as well. We were excited to be able to have family around again and looked forward to it.

At some point it was decided we would move the trailer to another town into a new mobile home park that was set in the hills with an amazing view. The park was so new there where hardly any other trailers in it. We got to pick which lot to take and I was amazed at how wide of a view of mountains we would get to look at every day.

**Before we moved to the new park something happened that had haunted me my whole life since.**

Of course much more happened when we moved to Colorado than I have told up until this point and more than I can really put into words at this time or in this book.

Even though there is so much being offered within this book as to things that have happened within my life there are whole levels of things that have happened that may be discussed in future books or one on one with the appropriate people.

> Something happened one day and in my memory I never went back to that school after that.
>
> Possibly I did and I do not recall, possibly it was summer vacation and we moved to the next trailer park before school started again.
>
> But it seemed like it happened on the way home from school. My friend and I were walking through the big open field of dirt with tumbleweeds and came upon some of the other boys from class who had dug an underground fort in the sand.
>
> There was a little hill to it and a hole on either side and they wanted us to go inside.
>
> I said no. The whole idea scared me and they kept persisting till my friend climbed in. I was standing alone listening to them call to me from underground telling me to come in.
>
> The other boys called me names and tried to taunt me to climb under and told me they had secret stuff down there.
>
> I finally pulled up the courage from inside of me and started climbing down into the hole.

I was shocked with how much space they had dug out down there, and magazines where all over the place. But, it was really scary to me, what if it collapsed?

I climbed out the hole on the other side and the other boys laughed while my friend pleaded for me to come back and hang out.

From above I extoled the dangers of that fort and that they should not be playing in it. I built up the courage to tell them that it was not safe and we needed to be smarter than playing in such dangerous situations.

The other boys laughed at me and made fun of me. I told them if they didn't come out I would go home and tell and their parents would force them to destroy the fort and never create another one.

They told me to go do that and called me names.

I recall starting to run home crying and upset. In the distance I saw my stepfather driving around the bend looking for me. When I finally got into the car he noticed I was all upset. He asked me what happened and I said nothing; and then blurted it all out.

In my memories of that experience there was as if a time warp of sorts.

I remember my father saying we would have to call the police and I remember feeling urgent that we should do it right away. I actually have a weird memory as if saying that he should use his cell phone, yet there were not cell phones back then.

*It's as if during my sense of fear and danger I was seeing into the future and that in emergencies there would be cell phones.*

*In that memory it was as if he knew I was having some sort of time shift sensory experience and I heard him say something about:*

**"I thought we left all this behind when we moved here".**

*The next thing I remember is standing next to a police officer as he congratulated me due to the fact I was such a mature boy to report such a dangerous play fort and that we should not as I knew build things like that.*

*He called me a hero, and told my stepfather he had a wonderful son and I just felt horrified to the whole experience.*

*I recall hearing something about the fact they couldn't find the fort and that the boys must have collapsed it and gone home since I had threatened to get them into trouble.*

*Though I have always had a fear that it actually collapsed in front of me and I didn't know how to deal with that and I would repress these memories in fear.*

**Writing this book is not only therapy for me but an example to show to others that we need to overcome fear itself.**

I had let go of all the fear I had inside of myself regarding those memories of the "sand fort" as I wrote about them.

In doing so as I quickly typed the paragraphs I felt the blockages of fear dissolve away and my insight into that afternoon many years back shifted as if the sands of time gave up its secrets and I saw very clearly all that I had feared so many years ago.

> *I stood there above ground begging my friend and the other boys to get out of the sand fort for it was not safe. I could hear the spirit realm starting to get louder.*
>
> *I started to hear more voices.*
>
> *I asked confused: "How many people are down there with you?"*
>
> *There was laughter at that – They asked me what I was talking about since I was just down there.*
>
> *The voices in my head got louder and started to caution me. I started to hear concern and feel worry as to what was about to happen – the voices started to caution me to step back and away from the sand fort.*
>
> *I demanded the boys get out –*
>
> *I was afraid for them and told them they were in serious danger and may die.*
>
> *One of the boys underground in the fort was laughing and saying how safe the fort was. He started to kick the fort from inside to show its strength and I could see sand dust lift from the dome of the hill from the impacts.*
>
> *I was hearing "another voice" as well from somewhere and the voices in my head where alarmed. The other voice was telling me to get closer to the fort. The other voice was trying to make me very mad inside. The other voice was not within me but I didn't understand from where it came.*

*I did not know how to get them out of the danger they were in. I told them as I was seeing the sand dust rise with each impact of the boy hitting it from inside that if they didn't get out I would destroy the fort myself to get them out.*

*Or at least that's what I heard it sounded like I said —*

*The voices of the spirits I was hearing inside myself were preparing for something large, there was a war starting and they were doing everything they could to protect us.*

*I sensed multiple realms of things starting to shift into place.*

*One of the boys hit the inside of the fort again —*

*This time the sand dust lifted and then sunk in as the fort collapsed onto them.*

*Within the realms of my memories I saw the boys come out of the fort faster than I could have imagined and spoke to me.*

*There was laughter, there was horror, and threats to my present and future life were leveled straight into my face.*

*I had the demon that was attached to one of the boys staring me straight in my face.*

*I now knew where that one voice was coming from, and it was straight from hell.*

*The demon did what they do best and spun a web of fear around me to lock me into a prison cell within my consciousness as to what had just occurred.*

*I saw spirits ascending, I saw ghosts. It even seemed like there was a horn of an angel going off all around me so loud I could not hear anything.*

I believe the more we let go of fear and its control over us, the more we free ourselves to life. The more we can allow light into our lives and our minds and consciousness the more we can grow and be free. Fear is a tool that others use against us. Even the media uses fear to get us to do what it wants and to believe the agenda it is selling us.

### Redwood Trailer Park

*The new trailer park was like a ghost town at first. We had no grass around the house, which just sat there seemingly out of place to me after we had it moved from the former town.*

*The summer weather gave me massive headaches, it felt like I could feel my brain shift and move in my head. Back then I didn't realize I only needed to drink more water due to the higher altitudes, no one explained that to me.*

*In fact I really felt pretty lost out there. We were told we had to go play outside and were often locked out of the house so we wouldn't sneak back in.*

*My school mates I left behind in Massachusetts mailed a big envelope of letters to me. It was one of their projects to write a letter to me and I was shocked by them.*

*It seemed like such a long time since I had even thought about those kids. I already was in the third school since*

> getting to Colorado due to all the moves. I really did not know how to emotionally respond to even reading the letters.
>
> I read some from kids I really didn't know and thought, they are saying these things, yet they really were not friendly to me when I was there.
>
> There were a couple letters from boys that really opened themselves to me, I saw the sincerity. Honestly I felt the actual love from them and I was shocked that they could say something like they did now when I was gone. I would never be able to be friends with them and why couldn't they have opened up before, in front of me, to let me know they could have been my buddies.
>
> Then there was the letter from my old girlfriend, and I felt so lost. Everything I had been through since we had moved to Colorado and now this, everything I lost staring me in the face, the magnitude was too great for me to bear.

What should have been a happy experience for me turned into an experience of feelings I could not deal with. There were too many emotions, too much sense of loss.

> I threw all the letters away and never responded to them.
>
> It was hard enough dealing with the kids in the new school and not fitting in. It was hard enough repressing all the things I would feel and sense that I did not understand what to do with.
>
> **The voices within my mind became less frequent and quieter, but the feeling of emptiness got stronger.**

*One morning as I lay in my bed, I overheard in my mind voices saying something to the effect, "Let's try again this time he may be ready finally". I suddenly realized my penis was hard.*

*Before this time I never recalled having what I would later in life learn is called an erection. I was a little freaked out by it, and even more so freaked out by what I heard and what that implied to me regarding things from my past. But the feeling coming from my waist area actually felt like a relief from the other feelings in my body. I was actually starting to feel something other than pain.*

**Having a family but not feeling a family -**

*My mother was drinking more and more at times and really wasn't happy. My stepfather would drink as well but was a rather quiet drunk, while my mother would get mad and go into emotional ups and downs of depression.*

*My mother and my aunt resumed a very strange bitter fight back and forth between them. One week they would be best of friends and the next after an alcoholic outburst on someone's part they were arch enemies again.*

*It always seemed strange to me that they would argue and disagree so much. After all I had heard the stories growing up how they really didn't have parents that they knew.*

*From what I was told they spent most of their childhoods in foster care as wards of the state. I heard horrible stories of the people that they had to live with. One woman actually hit my mother over the head with a hammer and would get drunk and slide down the hill with the neighbor kids in the winter clad only in a flimsy nighty with no underwear on.*

*These two sisters were split up from their brothers and lamented often of not really having a family as they grew up. Yet they fought together so much instead of realizing they had each other and they were responsible for creating their own families now.*

*After some months of all this going on and sadness of being away from other family, friends and home it was decided we would move back home to Massachusetts.*

*I was excited, yet confused, and I didn't know what this really meant. I knew I missed my step brother who really seemed like the only family I had in my life. I didn't know if this meant we would all move back together or where we would live.*

*It was explained that we would move back but my brothers would most likely not move back in with us since they had their places to live.*

*Calls were made and people spoken to, though my aunt and uncle were not moving back with us.*

*Even though it was an interesting place to go to, I was not happy in Colorado. I saw some amazing places but I had enough of the pain and wanted to go somewhere, anywhere if there was a chance that happiness might come from it.*

I had to learn that happiness can only come from inside. I needed to learn to overcome the things inside which did not belong, for happiness to grow and see light.

## Massachusetts

*Again, we got in the car and drove cross country but this time back to Massachusetts.*

You can queue the song "Massachusetts" from "The Bee Gees" within your mind if you know how that goes as you read this. That's the song I think of every time I think of the trip home.

*The part of the trip home I remember most, was arriving into The Brookfield's, the area we had lived in previously. It seemed as if something happened while we were away and someone mysteriously planted tons of trees.*

*The place seemed so overgrown with trees that we were all in shock from it. We were not gone that long to Colorado with the majestic views of the mountains that spanned for miles but arriving home we could not stop staring at the trees all around us. We had forgotten what the trees felt like.*

*We stayed a few days with some friends when we arrived. These people actually seemed to care about us.*

*They had found us an apartment to move into and had worked on cleaning it up. They even spent the time and money, painting the entry door, to help us with a fresh start.*

*It was what seemed like a big house to me. We had the first floor apartment and a couple with a son lived on the second floor above us.*

*It was called "Maple Street" in Brookfield, Massachusetts and was indeed lined with big maple trees. My elementary school was a five minute walk away. I would be entering the last year of elementary for the next year I would go to a local regional Junior High School.*

*It was a new start for me and could include possible new friends. Though, I wasn't getting ahead of myself since socializing was not my forte it seemed.*

It's hard to socialize and fit in when you sometimes hear or see things the other kids do not seem to. Feeling so much around other kids was not easy. Boys tended to want so bad to prove they were going to grow up to be a man they needed to dominate other boys in the process just like they saw the rest of society do.

**"It's a dog eat dog world" I heard a lot as I grew up.**

*I went to school and made friends. It was a small school. There were several girls that were very nice to me and I became friends with them.*

*The boys, well again, that was another story. There were a few boys that I could deal with being around but most of them I really didn't seem to have anything in common with. They just did not seem all that nice to me.*

*Again, I got picked on for not being how the stereotypical boy should be. One of the girls was tall and very pretty with long hair. I always thought she looked like the popular model Brooke Shields.*

*Another blonde girl always seemed to be there for me in class. I felt she really liked me, in fact possibly more than I was ready for. That seemed to cause a little friction at times. It seemed and felt to me that there was difficulty going on at her home. I resonated with her on what I felt inside of her, though I do not actually recall discussing those sorts of issues with her.*

*And then another girl, well she lived nearby and it seems decided for some reason that she would always try to force herself into my life. It was rather awkward at times.*

*My mother saw straight through her and disliked her for what she saw. For me she lived close by and at least it was a friend to have around at times. I tried my best to hope for the best for her. Though, I had to keep her at a distance when she got into what seemed like some sort of plotting with motives and agendas that didn't feel right to me.*

*One of the boys became my best friend. He of all my friends during my school years was the friend that I had for the longest. It was amazing to have a friend to hang out with and not feel like I was being judged or pushed around. I was invited over his house often and even got to go to Cape Cod with his family. We would stay at their family's house by the ocean. It was amazing to me.*

*My oldest brother Danny, who I really never knew very well, died during one of my school summer vacation periods.*

He died in California the month before he would have turned twenty. He was riding a Harley Davidson Chopper motorcycle with his girlfriend on the back of the bike. From what I recalled hearing - she was fortunate and survived the accident.

I remember being told by someone that even though he was not a "Hells Angel" they actually let him ride with them at times, due to how great of a guy he was. I thought that was curious thing to be told.

**Elementary School faded into going to Junior High School at this big regional school.**

It seemed so huge and took a while to not get lost in. It was a massive change from the elementary school. The school consisted of several towns' worth of other kids and each town seemed to have their own attitude come with them.

One of the towns which had the reputation for being "the better place to live" certainly strived to live up to its reputation with the children it produced. Many of them let the other kids know they were from the superior town or so they proclaimed to us in various ways of behavior.

The town I was from was a poorer town. It was known on the first day of school that your supposed rank of pecking order would depend on what town you came from.

Was Junior High a good time for me?

Well, as you probably can start to sense from the last paragraph it was one of the worst experiences I have had to deal with on a continued basis.

*In the beginning of Junior High I had a couple friends I would see out of school. Though not being able to get around to places since I didn't have a car was an obstacle. It seemed like too big of an ordeal to get many or any rides from my parents to places. Of course the fact I had no money stopped me from having a social life to do anything out of school as well.*

**In school it just got stranger as the years progressed.**

*I started seeing visions again. I wasn't pulling the reality of it fully out of my subconscious as to the fact this was something I had dealt with my entire life. Though, part of me was aware of how extreme the things I dealt with were. I felt totally alone within a crowd.*

*I knew I must have a lot to offer. I knew no one seemed to care. I had no idea of what to do about all of it. I was lost.*

**I started to sense plane crashes and other traumatic events in the world. I then would see them displayed and talked about in the newspapers I read in the school library.**

*It was a strange fact of awareness, and I knew there was more. Part of me was repressing the truth to it. I knew there was something different going on and part of me wanted to be who I actually was. Though, the part of me repressed was afraid.*

Even though I had a few friends, I really didn't talk to them about the real stuff going on in my life. In fact, as time was moving on at school, the distance increased between the friends I had.

One of my friends that only lived a couple streets away was told he could not see me anymore. His parents told him that I was not welcome over to his house ever again and he could never come over to my house.

I found this out because he snuck out of his house to tell me. I stood and stared at him. I could hear what he was saying but it was like his lips were moving, and I was hearing him but nothing was registering.

I was losing a friend. I was seeing that I was going to get lonelier than I already was. He said his parents told him that when I was older I was going to be a homosexual and would do things with men.

I was flabbergasted and asked if they had a vision of this. I wanted to know who told them this fact. I don't recall the whole conversation. I just know I was very confused and hurt. I knew I had no desires of that sort, I only wanted a friend.

He seemed so upset over it. I could barely think or feel. I was confused that he appeared to care about me as much as he was showing. I didn't actually realize that before because I was so lost in pain.

I realized once again that I was finding out someone cared about me more than I knew. And again was I losing them from my life.

**A strange thing happened many years later as an adult. I was working in my gardens in front of my house when a car drives up and a woman jumps out.**

> She came up to me and introduced herself as the sister of my friend from childhood. Even though she had changed a lot, I recognized who she was. I was curious and nervous as to why she drove up so fast and jumped out of her car to speak to me.
>
> She said that she drove by and saw me outside and felt she had to turn around and talk to me. Something happened that she thought I should know about.
>
> She commented that she probably shouldn't be telling me and that she might get in trouble for it later. She wanted to tell me anyways. She went on to tell me that her brother had gotten into some kind of accident at work and due to it lost his memory.
>
> She went on to tell me that when he recovered and awoke he didn't know who anyone in their family was.
>
> She went on to say that he didn't recall who his mother or father was or even who his own wife was. There was only one person that he could remember – and it was me.
>
> I stood there in shock, not sure what to think or even what to believe. Was this some sort of bizarre game someone was playing on me? She went on to tell me that he kept calling out to see me. No one would tell him if they knew where I was.

*The idea that this would happen was beyond my ability of dealing with at that time. I certainly didn't need to experience more pain by the judgment of that family.*

When I look back and consider his trauma of being denied my friendship. I can see that his family unknowingly caused a shift in ego states for him in painfully repressing and denying any friendship with me.

It would make sense to me that in a future physical trauma the memory of me, someone that had to be forcibly locked away in his subconscious, would arise again to be unlocked, within his current experience and trauma of consciousness.

While I don't think he loved me more, or in the ways he loved his wife, I think I may have touched his heart in ways he didn't realize in childhood.

I certainly remember several intense conversations with him when he wanted to play in his back yard and shoot squirrels with his BB gun. I demanded and declared that boys do not have to behave that way to be boys and the squirrels had a right to live.

I would state that he should view the squirrels as something special that wanted to visit his yard. There were better things in life than being a bully.

> **Somewhere in all this drama of Junior High School came the real trauma for me.**
>
> *I was in gym class standing at my locker ready to get dressed back into my school clothes. Suddenly I started hearing something very quiet, it was like it was deep inside of me, yet it wasn't in me.*

*It was like a calling, it was like I was being called. I was hearing my name and I was feeling as if I was being pulled or tugged to walk over to the coach's office.*

*It was very strange to me. I couldn't resist it, it was almost like a sirens' call of the mythical mermaids that would crash sailors onto the rocks. I slowly walked to the direction I was being pulled and ended at the door of the office, standing there dumbfounded.*

*I didn't know what to do, the door was closed and I could see in the window. The coach was sitting at his desk and I could see that there were others in the back room.*

*The coach waved to me through the window and said, "You can come in". As I did I don't recall if I just stood there or sat down on a chair under the window. But the memory seems to feel like I sat down and didn't say anything since I really wasn't sure what to say or what to do.*

*The coach didn't say anything to me. He just sat there with a newspaper in his hands. There seemed like something else was going on but I hadn't figured it out yet.*

*I had all sorts of emotions going on inside of me. I was feeling things inside I didn't understand. I was really not sure what I was actually feeling.*

*Then all of a sudden the coach reacted as if in a little pain and said something like "Ouch, watch the teeth" and I realized there was someone under his desk.*

*The coach moved back in his chair a little and I realized one of the other boys was actually under his desk performing oral sex on him.*

As strange as it may sound, I don't think I actually knew what oral sex was back then. I definitely saw what the boy was doing and did not know how to react. I was lost within everything I was feeling going on inside of myself that did not even feel like me.

This did not feel like a normal situation. The casualness of it had me confused.

The boy came a little more forward so I could see who he was. He made comments that he was shocked that I actually came in the room - that I "heard him calling me" and that "it worked". The coach was confused as to what he was talking about and started to tell him to be quiet.

At this point I felt in totally new territory. I wasn't sure what I just walked into, how I became aware of and entered into it to begin with. But I knew I wasn't sure what to do at this point, and I basically cascaded deeper into my thoughts to try to figure it out.

One of the other boys came out from the back room and the other coach followed him out with one of the girls behind him. I was shocked that one of the girls was in the boy's locker room. I was even more shocked that she was in the office when it seemed some pretty strange things were going on.

I knew right away from things that I had seen previously that she had a crush on the coach, who had been in the back room with her. He always seemed to flirt more than he should have with her as well. That part wasn't as shocking to me as the boy under the desk.

*The girl left and I really don't know if she knew the extent of what was going on in the room.*

**But then things got stranger.**

*The coach that was sitting down stood up and started to instigate something else taking place in the room. I really wasn't sure what was going on or where it was heading.*

*I knew that as oddly as it sounds I was getting attention and not getting picked on. I was feeling like I was starting to get included in something as opposed to getting excluded. I knew I liked the feeling of that even though I wasn't sure if I should be involved in what was happening.*

*I could feel energy inside of me, the empty space I normally felt inside was feeling something other than pain.*

*Yet, I knew I really wasn't interested in what it started to appear this coach seemed to have in mind.*

*My attention went to the other coach, he was tall or so I thought, good looking and in shape and I could feel the energy from his chest.*

*The energy from his chest is what really got my attention. His energy felt strong. It felt like it could protect. It felt like if I felt more of it I would feel safe.*

*I said something to these feelings and he was a little confused by it. He let me know he wasn't attracted to guys. He liked girls. I went deeper into my comment saying it wasn't about sex, yet he dismissed it.*

*At this point the other coach was now to my right and was talking about something. It was starting to feel like the room was spinning a little. As if once again, some multidimensional experience was happening. Things were being said, but some of the things being spoken, dealt with awareness of the future. I was confused how they would know these things, and my sense of time seemed thrown off a little from it.*

*It seemed like the coach wanted me to do something with the boy that had walked out from the back room. The boy was interested, yet I really wasn't willing to go there. Though I was feeling included and I liked this new awareness of not feeling the pain inside me.*

*I was being allowed to express myself when normally I always felt shut down. Though I felt as if they were playing a game on me and I needed to be careful since I was in danger with them.*

*The boy from under the desk came out and I seriously was not interested in doing anything with him. I had always felt something creepy around him. I was aware enough to sense he had just done something that led me into this experience, which I felt like I really shouldn't be involved in.*

*All I wanted was to feel the strength of the chest energy of the other coach. That was all I could think of and feel at that moment.*

*It was a yearning I did not recall feeling before, it was so close yet it seemed impossible and would not happen.*

*The first coach was now on the floor next to me. I believe I was still standing at this point, or maybe I was on my knees debating if I should do what I was just told to do to the other boy. I just knew I didn't want to do anything other than figure out all these things I was feeling inside of me. I was in a daze not sure what to do.*

*All of a sudden the boy from under the desk was watching the coach very intently as he was kneeling on the floor.*

*I couldn't really see the coach since I was in a daze and he was a little behind me. He responded to I think the boy from under the desk or maybe it was me he was talking to - but he said. "This is not what you think it is" and all of a sudden I felt a blunt poke at my anus as something tried to enter it. I then became totally un-dazed.*

*The boy from under the desk was behaving as if he was all jealous. He was trying to see what the coach was actually doing to me.*

*I stood and pulled up my pants. I declared very loudly something to the likes of, "This is wrong, you have no right to do this!" I went on with more and said something as "I will tell on you if you keep this sort of action up".*

*I don't recall fully what was said back, but it basically was regarding who are you going to tell and do you think they seriously would believe you.*

*In a way it was a preposterous thing to hear since there were enough people in the room as it was that were aware of what was going on. It was shocking because in the middle of it another male student walked in and had a look of total shock on his face and was yelled at to leave.*

*So how many people actually knew what was going on there? I was being told something that I just experienced that was very real and true, would not be believed?*

*I ran from the room to my locker to finish changing clothes, still incensed as to what just happened. I was so lost in being upset and knowing I was right. I didn't realize the freight train of future pain that was barreling from behind me.*

*Two of the boys from the coach's office came running after me. A third boy was picked up in the commotion who wanted to be part of the action. They came towards me from behind.*

*They jumped on top of me and hit and shoved me into my locker. As I write this I actually think I was literally pushed into my locker after they pummeled me as much as they felt they needed and shut the door on me.*

*My memory fades to black after I was attacked. It fades to so much pain I do not even remember the rest of that day or what came next.*

*I do remember that at some point after that and I assume it started the very next day I was jumped on and attacked pretty much every day for a very long time.*

*They always jumped on me from behind and I never seemed to know when it was coming. It would just seem to happen out of nowhere as if they were stalking me.*

*One of the times in the beginning while they were on top of me, hitting me in the back of the neck next to the top of my spine, I heard one of the boys say to me. "You know we are doing this because the coach wants us to beat you senseless".*

**In my adult life I have had neck issues ever since -**

*Yes, the coach wanted me beat senseless, so that I wouldn't have the sense to tell or to even remember what had happened to me. From those days on I had numerous nicknames from them. It seemed to spread as some others would chime in at times.*

*I became "The Faggot" in their minds and many other horrible names all through Junior High right into Senior High School.*

**It got so bad that I had days when I went to school and didn't know where I was.**

*I lost track of which class I was supposed to go to and several times walked into other class rooms. I vividly recall walking into a French class, with what must have been a total look of loss on my face. The teacher actually had me sit down and join the class stating there must be a reason I was there.*

*If I recall correctly I started going to that class often, not realizing what I was doing. I didn't learn any French. I just sat there dazed. I was feeling like it was somewhere safer than other places. I was living in an illusion during the class, not comprehending much of what was going on.*

*I even had myself convinced when they spoke in English about the class trip to France that I could actually go as well.*

*I started to forget what the code was to open my locker so I stopped bringing my books to most of my classes. When I did remember the code I sometimes realized I needed to bring all my books to all my classes in case I forgot again.*

> Then, I stopped remembering where my locker was. After all I would get beat up there, so of course my subconscious mind did everything it could to keep me away from my locker.

> My class coat with the school colors was stolen from me. It was thrown out one of the windows on to one of the roofs. It looked like it was destroyed before it was tossed out the window into the rain.

> I only know this because one of the girls I knew brought me to the window to show it to me. She told me it was mine.

> I was confused that it could be mine since the one I owned was in perfect condition. But of course I had no idea where it was. I thought my coat was in my locker but I hadn't seen my locker in days since I didn't recall where it was.

> After all I didn't know where I was most days during that time. It was as if I was not there, I was within a trance of pain and just attempting to move forward.

I would get up in the morning and go to school, struggle to survive and get through it not really conscious. I would somehow find my way home and then dream of different lives all night long until I had to get up again and do it all over again.

> The girl showing me the jacket said that my coat was taken from me since "they said" I wasn't worthy of wearing the school colors. I was told that they were saying I was the shame of the school.

> My best friend, the one I used to go to the cape with, was lost somewhere in this debacle as well. He came up to me one day at my locker; well actually it really wasn't my

locker that I was standing there trying to open. But rather mine was somewhere on the other side of the hall.

My best friend stood there and told me he was sorry but he couldn't be my friend anymore.

He told me that the other boys said they would treat him as they treated me if he did stay my friend. So he needed to stop being my friend. In fact, he claimed he needed to push me to prove it in front of them - so he was apologizing for what he was now going to do.

He said "I am sorry, I love you" then shoved me back into the lockers deeper into pain and confusion.

I was confused if he was telling me he was sorry that he loved me or if he was sorry for what he was doing. I was clinging to every moment in fear. I couldn't comprehend the bigger picture all around me.

Once again as would happen often in my life, I was being told I was loved and being left all alone at the same time. It seemed to compound my pain of loss and being alone even more.

The girl that showed me my class coat, told me that my best friend had friend stolen it. Stealing my coat was his initiation for showing and proving he was with the other boys.

There were days walking down the school halls that I recall. I literally pressed myself up against the walls as I walked. I probably only remember that because I overheard someone making rude comments about me. I heard them saying, I was starting to act like that other kid that hugged the walls as he walked down the halls.

I recall hearing a story about him. As a small child he walked into his grandfather's study right when his grandfather was blowing his head off with a gun.

Walking down or up all the flights of stairs at school got difficult for a time. It was as if my legs would not move.

My legs got so stiff as if they would fuse together. I would have to hold onto the railings and slowly go up the stairs or down them as if I was in slow motion. I literally was freezing in fear. I would sit in fear of the class bell that signaled the next class. How fast could I get there? Could I get there before I was jumped on? Would I remember which class it was I needed to go to?

Then one day a girl sitting behind me in one of my classes stated that she needed to leave class a couple minutes early due to the cast on her arm and suggested I carry her books for her to her next class.

She said "We will just get up, I will tell the teacher you are carrying my books because of my arm" and we will leave. I was shocked, could it be that easy? And it was.

She also had a key to the schools elevator and told me she would give it to me to use. She told me I should leave all my classes a couple minutes before the bell rings to get to my next class and that is what I started to do.

There was only one time anyone ever commented on it and otherwise it was like nobody noticed.

> The one time it was commented on was in the class the girl was in with me, but she no longer was there anymore. When she gave me the key to the elevator she also told me she was leaving the school. And, yes, another person showing me they care but at the same time they had to leave me.
>
> That one time it was commented on, as to "why does he get to get up and leave class early" was actually by one of the boys that would normally attack me. He stood up and asked it and I heard the teacher scream on top of his lungs. "Sit your ass back down and shut up" or at least something very much similar to that.
>
> I slightly turned in fear that the teacher was talking to me and I may be stopped. I saw the teacher actually go up to the student. He reached out grabbing him by the neck and started yelling at him even more. He asked him how he liked being treated that way.
>
> I ran fast from that room not sure if I was happy or if I was in so much trouble I would be dead after that kid sees me next.
>
> When I look back at that I realize how much everyone actually realized what I really was going through all those years. Though for some reason no one was willing to seriously help me but that one girl. Though, she could only do it her last days in the school strangely enough.

**Can pulling future awareness into the present to gain a sense of protection still be used to torment yourself?**

> One of those days leaving class I used the elevator and went to another floor of the school to get to my next class

> *early. I was walking in the middle of the hall all alone, or at least I thought I was all alone.*

When I think of this memory part of me always says to myself,

> *"Seriously, did this happen or did you dream this up as some sort of fantasy protection element for yourself?"*

As I type this part of the story I wonder. Will someone someday ask "him" if this is true and he will say, "No, I was never there and I never did that." Then will someone someday be able to then start convincing me that all these memories of abuse are not true.

Will I be abused again? Being made to believe as if I am living through the experience of that movie "A Beautiful Mind" where the man has this grand awareness of his life and then at one point is forced to come to deal with the fact it is all psychosis and none of it is real. Will the reality of what I have gone through be taken away from me again?

**But to continue "My Story"**

> *I walked into the main corridor of the hall way, where the staircase meets the adjoining hallways. Who walks by me and stops in mid stride? The rather tall stately looking man now stands in front of me. With a joyful heart he looks at me and says something like "Hi, How are you!" in this most endearing southern drawl.*

> *I felt so much happiness and determination and frankly it was love coming from him. He asked me the direction to a bathroom. We had a short interaction and I continued on not realizing who I may have just met.*

*I went looking for my next class not sure if I remembered where it was. I went down to the next floor and again bumped into the same man who said hello again with a big smile. At this point he was probably a little confused why this lone kid was milling about the school.*

*A little later on in the day we all had to go to the High School across the street for this big event. A politician that was becoming famous was actually on a jogging tour across the country "he was running for President in the future" and he had stopped at the school for a rest and to give a speech.*

*I thought to myself, do I need to go? Can I skip this? Where would I go since everyone else is going there? Like the hypnotized cattle being led to slaughter I followed the pack.*

*As I found my way into the school, there was a clear line of vision in front of me to that same man from earlier. He turns noticing me and says loudly in a genuine way as to the fact it is the total truth that "Hey, I Know You! And I want to be your President!"*

*William Jefferson Clinton the future President of the United States was standing there not only smiling, but he was pointing directly at me.*

*I was in shock. Everyone around me turned to look at who he was talking to and pointing at. I heard hushed comments such as "How does he know him?"*

*I stood there and exclaimed blankly in reply: "They won't let you be MY President".*

*Of course, I just sounded like a crazed kid saying that. And of course the coach was only a few feet away from me as were his pose of abuser. They all moved in closer in front of me. They separated me from the future President so I couldn't say anything more that might have come out of my mouth.*

*I started to turn and walk away knowing I could not speak nor explain what I really meant by that statement. I heard them saying to disregard me because I wasn't all there and was quite frankly crazed.*

Is that memory real? Did I meet the future 42$^{nd}$ President of The United States of America in the hallway of my Junior High, in the midst of the major daily trauma I was going through?

Did he actually "run" around various parts of the country years before he officially ran for President to seed and view the prospects of his run for office?

People I know do not recall that happening.

I have a therapist that believes I made it up within my mind that actual day by pulling forth my psychic awareness of him running for office and becoming President in the future.

My consciousness back then was so shattered and repressed within and without so many states of ego. My psychic awareness was pulling in things I could not comprehend and was on overload and moving through life on autopilot. The past and future seemed to be taking the place of my senses as they were askew.

*An interesting side note to this is many years later after a scandal was created around, something he was involved in he visited Worcester, Massachusetts. On his first public trip, after the news broke, much was made of the fact that Worcester was the city he would appear in and what might be said.*

*I had a store in Worcester in the big mall then. That day my friend Kevin and I were planning on going out for breakfast. One of the major things we talked about was would I bump into him again.*

*Somehow for some reason would he show up in my store? Would we meet him on the street in some way?*

*I wanted to go to Scano's Bakery for breakfast and visit our friends that owned it. Kevin didn't want to have to drive to that part of the city since there was so much going on with all the secret service and news people around.*

*I asked several times to go to Scano's –feeling like that's where we should be. And yet I relented and did as Kevin thought best, and went to another breakfast place.*

*As we sat down eating breakfast, watching the news on the television at the diner, we saw Scano's Bakery appear of the television. The President was having breakfast there.*

Whatever is the truth to those memories of that day in my childhood – regardless if Bill Clinton was actually physically there, being kind to a seemingly strange kid, he left a profound statement of kindness and love within me.

We are much more than the issues that may surround us. There is much more going on than is normally seen in the $3^{rd}$ dimensional realm.

**Do bullies grow up and raise bullies?**

When a child is a bully what happens if they do not grow out of it and awaken to kindness and love within them?

Do they then have children and raise them knowingly or unknowingly to be bullies as well?

> *I have a relative that went to the same school system as I did. She does not have the same last name as me and she was many years behind the years I went to those schools.*
>
> *Yet, I found out some years later that she was bullied as well all through her Junior and Senior High School years.*
>
> *One day in a heated discussion she and her mother yelled at me saying "It was my fault that this girl was picked on in school."*
>
> *I was confused as to what they were talking about and why I was being blamed for something I was not even around for.*
>
> *I do not blame them for yelling at me in their frustration. I understand very well the pain they were going through in dealing with the abuse that this girl had experienced.*
>
> *It is interesting to note though how in pain, anger and fear, people will transfer all sorts of issues over to others as if it is the other persons fault.*
>
> *I found out for the first time that this family member who I loved greatly was picked on verbally, emotionally and psychologically, and for all I know as well some physical harassment, due to the fact the other kids knew she was related to me.*

*Even though, I hadn't been in that school for a good amount of time, even though those other children had not been going to that school at the time either – their families had.*

*Their brothers and sisters had gone to that school. Apparently the great shame that I was to them, lived on in that school.*

*I was much more than just the class year joke. The kid that basically no one wanted to be around or know due to the fact of my strangeness, the rumors of who they thought I was might rub off on them.*

*I was more than ostracized the years I went to that school. I was a scarlet letter warning, for years after, for anyone not to be, like who they thought I was.*

*Most schools have mascots; I became that school's omen within their minds and spirit.*

**So the question still stands and the answer is:**

Yes, sometimes bullies do raise their own bullies and tyrants. Sometimes there are whole families of them, spreading their sickness outward to anything or anyone they can.

This knowledge is not judgment; it is clear awareness of fact. There is nothing to gain in holding grudges, when you are able to see the sickness and pain within others of what they manifest in their lives of living to harm others. Holding grudges only keeps the pains of the event within us. It is a reactionary display that is used to self-abuse ourselves again if we do not let it go.

Compassion and awareness is a lesson in of itself. For without compassion and awareness we suffer the deaths of others in a way some may not consider.

### I learned to overcome the abuse -

*When I grew up and was able to actually start discussing, the abuse that I suffered through my Junior and Senior High School years, I met various reactions.*

*The father of one of my "school friends" was enjoying commenting to me about his memories of the school those years back, so long ago. When I stated that I really did not have any good memories myself back then - he dismissed me by stating that I needed to let go of it. He did not want to hear of it. Keeping his illusions in place was more important than holding space for the reality of what I and others suffered through, not to mention the possibility of the fact that even more people were still being abused.*

*When I finally gained the courage to call the police, it took two phone calls to finally tell them my name. I was told he would be watched. I was told they "knew" about the other coach, and he got in trouble years ago, for what he was doing with the girls.*

*I was told since it was so long ago they couldn't do anything about it. Since no one else apparently was coming forward they could only watch.*

*I finally decided to call the school itself and called the guidance office to forewarn what could be going on.*

> *I was told by the lady on the phone, that it was not something she wanted to deal with. She did not want to know about it and in fact it was not the "type of counselor" she was.*

In situations like these many people do not want to get involved unless they think it affects them or their own family personally. A strange thing tends to happen and often has been shown very vividly in the press. In the last couple years the news broke regarding the repression of information of sexual abuse, over many years at a certain college.

Some people came forward in anger, directed at those that were abused. They objected to the truth and it being known. They objected due to the fact of how it affects them themselves and the fact it might disrupt their current season's sports game.

They could hold no compassion, for anyone involved but their own selves, for they were lost within the illusions of the culture they were in.

We still live within a society that abandons those that have been abused, in favor of not dealing with the situations. Thus in doing so they teach people not to come forward for knowing they themselves will be victimized even more. This will change.

This sort of behavior covers and emboldens the perpetrators sickness of abuse. Though, there is much more going on than mere dysfunctional people. Actual demons and entities are involved, within the spheres of drama, that play out within the lives of all those involved.

This as well will change. The new paradigm that is shifting through the universe into place is ascending all beings of light and less than light. There is no escaping the light of unconditional love.

**Mending Fences -**

We need to mend our fences and construct healthy boundaries of living for they are the holders of the vessels of our livelihoods.

Whether the fences are physical in our neighborhoods or energetic metaphors within our emotions they are sometimes needed regardless to decoration or intent to serve a purpose.

Sometimes others are not able to hold healthy space and in doing so we must construct our own fences just feet away from theirs. We need to be careful to not become a prisoner of any fence or boundary regardless to who's design. With an awakening awareness we can move beyond such needs and understand we are all in this together and in all clarity of truth come to the realization that unconditional love is the only buffer we ever really needed.

Garden fence at 'The Holistic Center'

## Turning Eighteen

*It was towards the end of July 1982 and I was over hearing talk of a family gathering which my mother was making a big deal about planning. My mother was inviting my aunt and uncle and cousins that we hadn't seen in a while. My sister that had previously moved out was invited and discussion on which day to make the big gathering ensued.*

*To me it all sounded like she was planning the special day to coincide with my $18^{th}$ birthday that was coming up. She discussed the various weekends upcoming. It seemed to me that she was pretending not to comment on my birthday to keep it a surprise. Though it wouldn't be a surprise for me, since I was well aware it was my birthday.*

*The date was finally chosen and of course it was August $8^{th}$, which in fact is my birthday. I spent the next couple of weeks looking forward to family coming together and celebrating my once in a life event, turning 18.*

*It had been decided to turn the big event into a picnic at "The Quabbin Reservoir" which is one of the largest man-made public water supplies in the United States.*

*It was created in the 1930's when the entire population of four towns had to be relocated. Hundreds of homes, businesses, a state highway, a railroad line, and 34 cemeteries were all moved or dismantled so that the* reservoir could be built.

Family I hadn't seen in years would be showing up for our family picnic on my birthday. My sister showed up at the house, in her own car, and handed me a present wrapped in silver tin foil and wished me Happy Birthday.

My aunt and uncle showed up right after. My aunt hugged me and gave me a card and I believe a little present.

My mom started reacting oddly as to why people were handing me things and when I stated: "well it is my birthday" figuring that at this point the surprise was out in the open. My mother replied "No, it is not."

Confused but knowing indeed it was my birthday, I figured that possibly she was not pleased that presents were given to me early and that they should have waited until I saw my surprise cake. I decided to travel with my sister to the location of the picnic.

The day evolved and everyone was having a fun time yet I was confused. It was as if it was not my birthday and no one wanted to discuss it.

After we ate and no cake arrived my sense of loss increased and my confusion lingered since I knew indeed it was my birthday, and it was my $18^{th}$ birthday.

Yet, not only was it not being honored, I was being told I did not know what I was talking about. My mother flatly stated that of all people she should know when it was my birthday and it was not that day.

*I left the picnic with my sister early. Of course now I realized it was not my birthday party but the gathering just happened to be on my birthday.*

*As I look back I realize another state of ego and consciousness was forming to repress the pain of that day within my mind.*

*Life was a big blur of pain for me. On all sides I felt like I was not allowed to be who I was. Though, I really did not even know who I was. I wasn't even sure of what I was feeling. My sensory awareness was showing me things I did not understand and it was as if everyone was involved in a huge lie and no one would openly discuss it.*

*It seemed like everything was layers of secrets. There were times it seemed people were actually trying to once again coach and teach me in coded ways how not to let on what I actually saw and knew was happening all around me.*

*I would pay attention to the little psychic visions and information I would telepathically receive. When I saw the plane crashes or the earthquakes a day or so later reported in the newspapers or on TV, I would just quietly force it from my mind that this all could not be real.*

*I was in the last year of High School and was determined to finish school as early as I could and get away from all the abuse I was going through there. I knew I had enough credits in my classes that I could actually leave in January and still be able to graduate in the spring. Even though of course there was no way I would go back for the graduation ceremony.*

Getting out of that school and the horrors I experienced was all that mattered. I survived every day to get to that last day with no intention to ever return.

I had no idea what I would do after high school. I had no money for college and after everything I was going through up to now in school, all alone with no one to talk to, there was no way or even ability to conceive for me that I could go on to college.

My family did not even seem to be supporting me in any options for what I should do after I graduated from High School.

My mother was too lost in working towards her recovery from alcoholism, and recovering from her own horrible childhood to be able to help me. My step father had said previously that I could not discuss any of my worries or concerns with her. Her own therapist had instructed her to offer me "tough love" which was the therapy rage of the 80's for people with kids they didn't know what to do with.

Of course I could not discuss my feelings or what was going on in my life at school with my stepfather. There was a dark family secret that I knew was being kept of what he had recently done himself that had torn the family and my mother apart even more. He was not safe to confide in.

I had no money to speak of. I had no car and there were no prospects I could see for even getting a ride anywhere to get to a job, if even I could find one.

When I turned 18, the child support checks that had been coming each month, since I was a toddler, started coming to me instead of my mother.

*I actually was able to start getting haircuts again. For a while I was cutting my own hair since I had no money for haircuts and didn't normally have a way to get to any place that I could get my hair cut at to begin with.*

*I was a prisoner within my emotions at school and when the school bus brought me home I was a prisoner in my room in pain hoping that the next morning of school would somehow never arrive and I could extend the meditations I found myself in each night to the point past the abuse I felt all around me.*

*"Tough Love" was a concept that did not seem like love at all to me. I wasn't doing anything wrong to begin with. I just did not realize any way out of the situations of abuse I was under from pretty much everyone in my life.*

*I knew my mother loved me deep down inside. Though, I knew my mother could not help me nor did she have the ability to offer me the love and understanding I needed. She was still attempting to overcome a childhood of abuse and pain herself.*

*She made me a present at a ceramics class of a football clock. She was oblivious to the fact I had no interest in sports. She had no clue that sports for me, was a reminder* of the daily abuse I suffered in school. I stood there holding that clock aware of her excitement that she worked hard to make me a gift. But deep down inside of myself I wanted to smash it to bits. That clock was a reminder of all the times of abuse I suffered in school and no one cared enough about me to know. They were all lost in their own issues.

Later in life I would understand the concept of "tough love" was to not help people if you were enabling them to do things that were not healthy for them. If you were not helping them to begin with, then throwing the tactic of "tough love" at them makes no sense. It is as if you are taking an abused person and punishing them for the crimes of those that abused them in the first place.

**I had moments of hope in those last few years of High School.**

*One day as I was walking home, rather I should admit running home in embarrassment. I was being laughed at and taunted due to my hair was pretty wild looking since I couldn't afford to get it cut. Some in fact younger kids, as sad as that is, felt the need to point it out.*

*Somehow in the midst of that emotional pain, as I was running home I saw a wonderful old lady in her expansive gardens tending to them. All I could think of was that she was like a grandmother that I never had. I abruptly stopped and asked her, while I was still half in tears, if I could help her in her gardens.*

*While, my intention was not that I was looking for a job, indeed I was only looking for a friend.*

*Yet, Mrs. Gavitt would not only serve as a friend and as a grandmotherly figure, she would also offer me a start to financial help in a small way by paying me for the time I got to spend with her. To this day I cherish the times in her gardens and sitting in her kitchen having cookies and tea when most kids my age were doing other things.*

*Mrs. Gavitt was playing grandmother to the small emotionally disturbed boy inside of me. I sincerely believe from things she said to me at times that she was waiting for me in those gardens for many days before I did finally show up. That day shocked her, that of all the days she patiently waited for me to find her, that I would do it in the midst of such drama.*

*I sincerely believe that she foresaw me entering her life and the role she would play in holding space for me. In a way she has always felt like a secret ambassador of god to me.*

*Before the day came that I finally finished High School I had been spending weekends at my sister's apartment as a way to escape the pain of being at home. Though, all those wonderful times away from the turmoil of home seemed to cause me more confusion.*

*On one hand I felt safer but on the other it was as if there was a game being played of teaching me something but it had to be done quietly and in the dark almost as if "others" may see.*

*I started to feel like I was being instructed to hide what I was really sensing. I needed to behave more like a sheep, acting like I didn't know and keeping the secret of awareness or I would be in deep danger.*

*No one was to know. People did not let on the things they were aware of due to the fact "some authority" would take action against them.*

*All this was cautioned to me by those who would actually later hand me over to the authority of a mental ward themselves, due to the fact they could not comprehend the truths. Thus they could only perceive that I must be the one insane.*

*Whether I was imagining it or not, it seemed like I was being coached to lay low and keep my head under the radar otherwise "they" would come after me.*

*Once again, all the times it seemed I experienced as a kid, growing up with strangers walking by me and whispering the phrase "shh, don't tell or they will come for you" was coming back to me.*

**Through my sister I met my father once again; I hadn't seen him since I was a small child.**

He didn't feel like a father figure to me. Once again I felt embarrassed and short changed by another man who I thought was supposed to represent a father figure for me in life.

I discovered that he could not even read or write and I was numb to that reality.

The story I heard was that as a small child for some reason his parents sent him off to live with nuns and that is where he got his schooling.

*According to him his schooling really didn't amount to much other than working for the nuns doing cleaning yet they would allow him time to be creative and draw and paint.*

*Those stories even confused me more due to all the fragments of visions, experiences and whispers of prophecies I had had in my life and my understanding of what religion was.*

*My father asked me what I was going to do after I graduated and I told him I hadn't a clue.*

*If he felt a fatherly duty or a chance to step in and help me, I do not know, but he invited me to move in with him, his current wife, and her son after I graduated and they would help me find a job.*

*I don't recall how many months I lived with them, but I do recall some very extreme psychic experiences as well as just plain strange occurrences. Finally my step brother invited me to move in with him in North Brookfield, Massachusetts. I suddenly felt like I might be saved, from the bleakness of where I was heading.*

**Those psychic experiences are so extreme that I am not even willing to go into them in this current book.**

*As I got older, I started to become aware of what would appear to be my past lives. (If indeed past lives are real) I realized that some of those experiences, at my fathers, dealt with those past lives and other people's awareness of them. A connection to a prophecy was quietly spoken of.*

*I never really felt love from my father even though I believe he did tell me he loved me. I don't think he knew how to express it and maybe he didn't fully understand love himself. The fact that his son was not the usual type of son I believe often left him unsure what to think or feel around me.*

*The move to my step brothers was another reach out from the man that was not actually a blood relative of mine but would continue to be more of a family to me than anyone else that actually was a blood relative in my life.*

*He did his best to help me even though he himself was working through dealing with overcoming a very hard childhood.*

*Somewhere, in the midst of the ensuing time at my step brother's house, life times of drama played out.*

*My visions got stronger and I got more lost in what was real and what was seemingly not. It seemed everyone was paying more attention to the illusions and not to the things that seemed more real even though they seemed so very strange. And again much of this I may have to explain (if I ever do) at another time and possibly within another book.*

*I started studying and reading books like "Autobiography of a Yogi" by Paramahansa Yogananda and "The Holy Science" by Swami Sri Yukteswar who was the guru of Yogananda.*

*I started collecting all sorts of books on consciousness and opening to one's spirit. I started to once again go within and recall things from my childhood. Abilities that I had seemed like they were beyond what appeared to be the standard awareness of those around me.*

*My states of consciousness were opening. Repressed memories unleashed their confusion and their light of knowing as I struggled to go to work and deal with everything going on around me.*

*After a while I stopped going to work and just stayed in my bedroom reading and meditating and became a recluse. My step brother struggled with what he should do for me.*

*He offered me time to just be and knowing that I was trying to overcome things even he couldn't comprehend.*

*Many horrible things happened including being quietly tormented and harassed by one of my step brother's friends that came around the house often.*

*Once again I was being pushed around and tormented by someone that decided for whatever reason, that I had no right to live.*

**When my step brother was not around this person often would even threaten my life and tell me he would kill me.**

*I seriously believed he would kill me if he had a chance. If he thought he could get away with it, he would. I considered that might not even matter if he just was mad enough. I witnessed him literally push his girlfriend down a steep flight of stairs in anger. When my brother scrambled after the girl to help her she denied the fact that she was pushed and claimed she fell.*

*Obviously she was just as frightened of him as I was.*

*I recall a period of time when I stayed in my bedroom only to leave to use the bathroom or find food in the kitchen and then hurry back. I longed for when my step brother would be home so I could feel safe in the house.*

*Many years later this person would show up again in my life. I was helping a friend in her store and he realized I was there. He thought he knew her enough to speak to her boldly so he told her that she needed to fire me. He claimed she needed to get rid of me - that I did not even have the right to be alive, since he said I was gay.*

*She told me this due to her horror of the realization that people like him thought this way. Her own son had just come out to her weeks prior, and she realized more fully what he was going to have to deal with his whole life.*

Now if you remember in the beginning of this book, the story of my life I had mentioned at five years of age. I had visions into many portions of my life. I had seen the fears, the pains the trauma and torture I would endure due to the beliefs of others.

I saw ahead before I even knew what sex was that I would be hated and abused for being what others would call being "gay".

I saw that I would be ridiculed during my Junior and high school years for the assumption of being gay, even though I was being beaten up daily for NOT having sex with the male teachers or the other boys.

I will state here that I do not think the male teacher was gay or was he bisexual. He was married with kids and deeply disturbed as well as a predator. Sex was the tool he used to control and to abuse others with.

I didn't even have actual "sex" until I was in my twenties - other than having experiences as a young boy sleeping over at someone's house on their sofa and empathically feeling the husband and wife have sex as if they both were inside of me.

> *I recall lying there trying to sleep and all of a sudden I felt my insides stir. It felt like I was coming alive from within - my whole body was tingling and then suddenly I could feel the rocking back and forth in me of the man in the other room having sex with his wife.*

> *I could feel her emotions with each stroke inwards and the pleasure with each stroke off of her. I was lost within with the energies and it just kept going until I could take no more and I quietly yelled out "enough already will you finish!"*

> *Within moments he was on the sofa asking me what I just said and I tried to explain I was trying to sleep and I couldn't because of all the emotions of what they were doing in the other room.*

> *He was floored and flabbergasted and tried to take in the comprehension of what was going on.*

> *All I wanted at this point, from being overwhelmed from all the emotion I had experienced for the last twenty minutes and NOW all this emotion of his shock, yet wild awakening of awareness, was to be hugged and fall asleep being protected.*

> *I of course had to sleep alone even after being part of an empathic three way, which for me, was not satisfying in the end.*

**And then there was the experience that I was forewarned of by "the voices in my head" when I was around four years old.**

I was walking down a small hill in the center of town with my brother. I stopped and I don't know if I heard it from out of his mouth or I heard it from spirit following me or where it came from but I heard "what was going to happen when I was older with that other couple".

I didn't comprehend it fully at the time as to "what it was" and it was not explained to me at four years old. It was more of a shock wave of awareness I felt from something that had not yet happened.

It was during a period in my teenage years that I felt so very alone and was aware I was in the process of losing the only support; I thought I had at the time, for friends.

A couple I knew took me out to say goodbye. We had a nice time hanging out and then they wanted to say goodbye and give me a "bear hug". She was in the front and him from the back.

It was just a hug or so it seemed. Clothes of course were on and it was just a hug of deep love.

Though, something else happened – energetically I entered her (or rather she opened the tantric way and allowed me within) and from the back side still fully clothed, energetically he entered. All I can say was that it was an energetic vision of ineffability.

As a small child before I even comprehended what sex was, I was already facing the awareness and the trauma of the fact I would live a life of being abused by other people's reactions to who they "thought" I was.

So again, I wouldn't actually have sex with anyone other than these strange experiences I have just mentioned until I was late within my 20's. Yet all that time I was being tormented and judged and accused of things I hadn't even done.

When it comes to definitions of sexual categories it is clearly understandable to me why I would sexually consider myself bisexual over any other option – possibly in a more advanced world Omni sexual might work better.

What I do find rather interesting is why others take so much uninvited interest - exert so much pointed energy within the personal business of another's sexuality to begin with.

It is as if they have a deep dark fetish and desire of their own sexual energy and instead of addressing those things, they transfer all their sexual energy into a repression of another's life force in a way that they then gain some sort of twisted satisfaction of control.

Instead of using their energy to raise their consciousness within the ascension of their living, they act out their own perversion claiming it to be another's.

Quite frankly I feel the energy of the universe stream through me and that energy is male and female - that energy is the sexuality of being love and of being life itself.

When I work with clients I often notice and sense much about their sense of their sexuality and any issues they may have surrounding it. I often meet people that have sex lives that are more of a reaction from their life experiences rather than their own real sense of attractions and desires.

Often people's sexual desires are controlled by the mind sets of others that have been instilled within them.

I've met men that consider themselves gay, when in fact from what I can sense, they are really playing out that role because of the fact they have a psychological aversion of women, which does not permit them to have feelings towards them, other than the pathology they have reacted into.

I've also met men that consider themselves "straight" when in fact their spirit calls out to me for much more than a friendly relationship. Yet they themselves cannot allow their physical body or their psychological constructs to even admit their true feelings and live in an illusion to even them.

I have met some heterosexual men that have become confused when they realize they are sexually attracted to me. I have had to teach them that in fact it is not me they are attracted to.

In these times of their confusion I have had to teach them that they are only attracted to the fact I have a certain energetic control and awareness of the sexuality of being and its abilities of freedom and movement throughout my body.

What they are actually attracted to is the fact their own sexual energy is craving to be set free and reach the heights of energetic awareness, of higher dimensions, they know they can sexually feel when they are close with me.

I have wondered if indeed I had grown up in this life feeling protected by a strong male figure and as well had male friends as a child that were able to share in a healthy manner and not of the "be the top dog or else" mentality if I would have craved as much male bonding energy support as I did in my young adult life.

That is not to say I believe it to be the case, nor do I believe in all cases it is nurture versus nature. I also do not believe for everyone that it is not a choice or that it is a choice.

I wonder how many people will be confused by such a multidimensional type of thought process as that.

I also wonder how many people will comprehend how their own judgments and opinions can affect others and how all the hatred and misunderstanding of sexuality in the world is creating many of the actual issues some are judging.

When you live a life of seeing, witnessing life from many dimensions, including from the heavens at times – life appears much different than some would want you to easily believe.

> **As a small boy I did not feel protected, I did not feel safe.**

> *As a small boy I cried out within my soul for a father to protect me. I saw into the many stages of the boy to man that I would become and realized I had to become more of a man than most men would ever dare allow themselves to be, just for myself to survive a life I didn't even want to be within.*

There are things within the past of this life I would change if I could, but sometimes I wonder if that is part of gods quest for me, to realize it is fine, if I do not portray being perfect within this realm.

> **I AM perfect within the eyes of god for I do believe.**

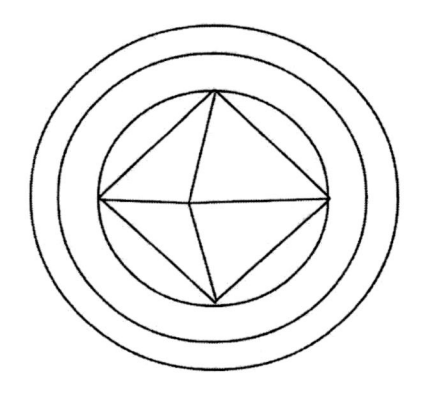

# Altea (ahl – tay – ah)

Sacred Space Creation

Courtesy of: BePeaceNow.org

# The Violet Flame Awakening

In the midst of all the emotional pain and torment of not knowing where to go for safety, or how to find safety in the world I found myself in, the only place that I knew to go was deep within me.

I was meditating more than I was sleeping and I barely left my room.

I was a recluse for how many months I do not even recall. I read books that I would order through the mail and was determined to overcome, within me, whatever it was that was wrong.

I didn't want to live in the world that I felt all around me. I thought the deeper I went inside myself I could run away from it.

**It didn't feel like I had any other direction to go.**

I didn't want to be part of the world. I didn't want to have an effect on anyone and I didn't want anyone to have an effect on me. All I seemed to know up till this point was pain, confusion and not being accepted from others.

> *In that mindset I was lost within - humans seemed like a horrible species to me.*

*It seemed, my whole life, until then was confusion and torment. Confusion and torment of things I saw that would be in my future that I didn't understand. Confusion I felt of how to survive and if I could get out of the way of it all.*

*I knew I was not who I presented myself to be and I knew that if I tried I would not be allowed to be.*

*It always felt like something huge was being kept from me as if I had an inheritance that others knew about but would not allow me to have. Instead it seemed they themselves were reaping the benefits of it all.*

*As strange as it sounds from all the visions and experiences I had during my life, I felt as if I held a secret that would change the world. Yet the world would not allow me to show the light that I knew was inside of "us all" because of what it would show the world and what the world was hiding.*

*Memories of old prophecies floated in and out of my various states of consciousness and what my role was within them and the danger I was in because of this.*

*One day during that time I lay in bed within meditation in the dark of the evening. I was the only one home. With every ounce of life and passion within me inwardly I threw it all upwards to the heavens crying out deep inside of me, "WHY?"*

**I demanded within my soul to know WHY?**

*I had mustered the audacity and demanded the attention of god to explain to me right then and there every single*

> *question I had within me and the pain I harbored for so long. "WHY?"*

**In what years later I would understand to be considered "A Violet Flame Awakening".**

> *I was with my passion exalted and thrown into the heavens energetically as if I was a fountain of light. Time and space did not seem to exist, I seemed to be one with god and everything was one.*
>
> *I was speaking to god and god was speaking to me, yet god was me and I was god it seemed.*
>
> *My questions and the answers of god seemed to ask and answer all at the same time.*
>
> *I was a fountain of pure light and the words, if indeed they were actually words, were light as well.*
>
> *Everything was asked and answered; I was within and was the fountain and light of god.*
>
> *The relief, the joy, the peace and love I felt I did not recall ever feeling before in this lifetime. I was in heaven.*

I believe there existed a time before this current form of civilization, many thousands of years ago, that the "Spirit Beings" that predate what we now consider human kind were in tune with the universe much more and regularly "spoke with god" in ways that the average person now does not comprehend.

Scientists talk about how the brain has grown over thousands of years and have labeled various "new" portions of the brain which I feel have limited and altered the conception of god and the spiritual connection in modern times.

I believe that we are in the process of an integration of our understanding of the brain and our energies of consciousness. In fact a new consciousness which is actually housed within the heart, and not the brain, is emerging to take humanity to the next level of being. (Or possibly back to where we actually are).

There are many modern day writers that attempt to explain and teach about the dimensions of consciousness. Some write from their own studies of meditations of consciousness while others write from what they call "channeled knowledge" from higher dimensional sources.

**One of the books I suggest my students and friends read on this subject is "Alchemy of Nine Dimensions" by Barbara Hand Clow.**

Most people including Barbara Hand Clow freely admit there are possibly more than Nine Dimensions. Though, at this time that is pretty much all the "human mind" is able to comprehend and process if indeed it can do that.

Briefly stated, to help understand the memories I am speaking of, within this chapter I will discuss a very scaled back even generic version of my own personal integration of what I believe these dimensions partially consist of and how they can be comprehended.

I do suggest reading "Alchemy of Nine Dimensions" for a deeper more precise understanding.

Having a working understanding of "chakras" which are the vortices of our energy bodies, as well the energy bodies of the earth and the cosmos, helps within this as well.

**1st Dimension** - The iron core center of the Earth itself - The "Root Chakra" of our universe and the energetic connection to our own physical body which connects from our feet to our tail bone area.

**2nd Dimension** - The layers of the Earth - The "Sacral Chakra" of our Universe which are the energetic elemental materials that are used while grounding to the Earth from the higher dimensions to manifest a third dimensional physical body to be used as a vessel and container for the energies of the higher dimensions.

This includes the energetic materials that our parents bring forth up their own containers to mix with the spiritual energy of their sexuality that creates another human vessel of which we encounter as our own physical vessel.

**3rd Dimension** – What is considered the realm of our physical bodies (vessels/containers) - The "Solar Plex" – Our will of existence - The energetic holder of the physical material that makes up this book you currently hold.

**4th Dimension** – An umbrella of sorts that veils the space between the third and fifth dimensions - It is currently built up of group thought processes, the "rules" of religions, the aspects of the workings of modern media control and all sorts of dualities and polarities of human history. A place of "Dark Archetypes" as it is the home of the dark forces that work to suppress the awakenings to the higher dimensions. One might consider it in a way the "Lower Heart Chakra" of the planet and cosmos with its condition of health/compassion being equal to the condition of the elements of light that are able to transcend in and out of this dimension.

But is it? Is this dimension currently in a major state of change with the shifts of the old paradigms dissonance of the new paradigm setting into its position? The answer of that may be in your own hands of creation.

**5th Dimension** – The Higher Heart chakra – a field of light which expresses the workings of the higher dimensions into the lower dimensions. It is all about creating with "thought" while holding 3rd dimensional reality in a field filled with compassion, forgiveness and unconditional love.

**6th Dimension** – The Lens of The Mind's Eye of the Universe Chakra - which interplays and overlays with the physical mind's eye of people- Sacred geometry of our purist image of the third dimensional form – As above so is below.

**7th Dimension** – The Cosmic Sound of the universe which creates 6th Dimensional images by the vibrations of said universe.

**8th Dimension** – The light and color itself of the universe from the divine mind of what some would call "god", which itself creates the vibrational sound of the 7th Dimension.

**9th Dimension** – Is a Creation that emanates from the center of the galaxy as waves of time. Which then interact thru the lower existence and personal power to the core of the Earth and our gravitational pull down and upwards thus co-creating the dimensional aspects we consider being here in the now.

**Back to: "The Violet Flame Awakening".**

> *During the visions which in a way were like a holographic enfoldment of the space of no time or possibly all time - I witnessed many things.*

*Towards the end I was aware I would have to go back to my life on Earth. I became aware again that I would face horrible pain and suffering not only of my own but of others.*

*I did not want to go back yet I knew I would have to. I feared the loss of the knowledge and awareness I had experienced. I feared losing my mind again.*

There is a romantic comedy film from 2004 called "50 First Dates" starring Drew Barrymore and Adam Sandler in which the character Lucy (played by Drew) has a certain form of amnesia and cannot remember the character Henry (played by Adam) no matter how many times they meet.

Lucy keeps meeting Henry each day yet does not remember him the following day since she only has the capability of remembering her life up until a specific time and does not retain any new memories after she goes to sleep at night.

The first time I saw the movie I was affected by it in a way that I cannot clearly describe. The pain I felt during the touching portions as she would lose her memory would flood back my memories of the pain, of this point of this vision when I realized I would keep forgetting and losing awareness and struggle with every ounce of my life to regain the light I had experienced.

Memories cascaded back, from all through my life, of times I repressed memories due to the pain I was in.

Watching the movie I had a screen of awareness play out in my mind of all the levels of ego states I would forget and then remember at seemingly random moments of time.

I had been having many strange and epic style visions around this time. Some of them almost seem to all blend together within that space of no time or all time that it is a strange experience to try to distinguish and discern the placement of the timing of various portions and streams of awareness.

There was a point, within one of the visions, I found myself as if standing way above the earth within space looking down at the planet. I was enthralled in the fact I could see so much. I put a bee line of attention in direction of my awareness looking for something within the time and space of the planet.

I was hearing something that was drawing my awareness to it at light speed.

At the same time, I could hear as if behind me, whispers asking, "How is he able to do this?"

Within my vantage point thru time and space, as I was consciously high above earth, with my physical body down on the planet itself somewhere within the year 1983 I located what I was being drawn to. It was many years beyond where my 19 year old body lay.

I was seeing into a future, where my future friend Kevin, that I knew as a child I would someday meet, was explaining to one of his friends that he no longer could believe in god anymore for his pregnant sister was dying of a brain tumor.

I recall defiantly stating that I would not allow that to happen. I would meet him as I had foreseen and I would make sure that he did believe in god.

*I heard as if from behind me that it doesn't have to be this way. I barely listened and did not listen since I was so determined that I would be there for Kevin within the future.*

# The Descent

I sit here starting to write this chapter, knowing all along while working on this book that I did not want to write this portion.

For a time I literally thought I could skip telling the story of these memories and then realized I had to let it unfold even though it might be painful for me to do so.

This book is a multidimensional undertaking – it is therapy for me and at the same time I know it will be therapy for many other people that may read these pages and learn much about their selves at the same time.

It is a doorway for me to open to show others there is nothing to fear. While there may be much to overcome in life we are able to do so and there is a whole realm of heavenly beings assisting us much more than we possibly know about within this, the $3^{rd}$ dimension.

Even though this chapter is in the middle of the book it is one of the last chapters to be written since I have held off on writing this.

While writing this book I have had memories flood back to me regarding this chapter and it is good I have waited to write for this purpose to allow what should be within these pages to appear.

It is the last week of April 2012, as I approach telling this portion of memories; I am sitting in an apartment I have rented for the week in Lily Dale, New York.

I came to Lily Dale to get away for the week to finish up the hardest part of the book and hopefully go home to West Brookfield, Massachusetts with only editing left to do.

For those not aware – Lily Dale is one of the largest, if not largest, Spiritualist communities in the world from the "Spiritualist Religion". I am sitting in an apartment in a very little town surrounded by mediums that live in most of the other houses.

Lily Dale is a gated community and has a "season" each year where people come from all over the world to visit to take classes from world renowned psychics/mediums and teachers.

An interesting fact is that Susan B. Anthony (2/18/1820 – 3/13/1906) A prominent American Civil Rights Leader who played a pivotal role in the 19$^{th}$ century women's rights movement to introduce women's suffrage into the United States, was born and lived here as well.

### The Descent -

*I did not realize as I was energetically falling from the higher dimensions back into the 3$^{rd}$ dimension after the "Violet Flame Awakening" what I would encounter for many years afterwards of pain and suffering.*

*But then, possibly I did know and that is what I saw, as I was falling into the chaos of humanity getting lost and losing parts of my awareness in the process of it all.*

*The most striking thing I saw and retained, as I fell, was an encounter with my future friend Kevin's sister who was ascending upwards at a point as I was descending downwards into the chaos.*

*Within the images and feelings of what I was seeing, as we met, in the between worlds for lack of a better word right now, she handed me a set of keys that belonged to her family and I was given instructions.*

*I suddenly realized in one hand it seemed I held the keys to my future friend's family and in the other held the keys to my own family and myself.*

**The message of instructions echoed thru my being as I was falling. Somewhere on the decent I realized I had lost both sets of keys as I was hitting the earth at a speed of light (or possibly a speed of "loss of light") I cannot fathom.**

*The confusion I had for what was real or what was imagined or better yet what I was trying to comprehend and understand from what really is in life was much more severe the weeks after this experience.*

**I should note at this point:**

This all was taking place within the 19th "earth calendar year" of my current life. Even though it appears that I energetically, spiritually met my friend's sister, in the higher realms, as I was descending and she was ascending, she did not actually physically pass away till many years later. This I believe is a very clear example of the realities of the eternal now.

I have often wondered what Kevin's sister actually knew while she was alive since I never met her within the "physical realm". I have wondered if she had visions of me. Did she, at whatever age she was, when I was 19 become aware of me within her dreams?

I have wondered why she had a brain tumor and even if somehow it was related to me. What was really meant by "It doesn't have to be this way" as I had heard from behind me? Way up in the higher dimensions.

Why couldn't I have understood the mysteries of "spiritual healing" sooner? Could I have somehow saved her from the brain tumor? And what was the real message, I was supposed to have learned to prevent it from happening in the first place?

Or was it meant that it was not my responsibility to make sure Kevin believed in god - or was it something else?

> *There was no physical person around me that I knew of that I could go to and explain what was going on with me. I felt totally lost – alone and frightened more so than I could ever explain within these pages. It was purely ineffable.*
>
> *People now scared me, more than ever before in my interactions with them. It was as if I was seeing something but had no way to describe what I was seeing nor had any form of perspective around it to be able to separate from the trauma all around me and my own being itself.*
>
> *At some point I was invited to join the youth music group at the Congregational Church in the town I was living in. Even though I told them I couldn't sing they told me it didn't matter since it was more about spiritual community than my ability to sing.*
>
> *I finally felt like I might have friends even though I didn't feel like I fit in.*
>
> *The three people in charge of the group made an extra effort to show they cared. It helped since not long after*

*joining the group it was obvious I did not fit in. I was not understood. In fact I was severely misunderstood in my immature attempts to fit in.*

*The group was disbanded, which had more to do with the fact that was the easiest way to get rid of me, which seemed to be their problem, yet a horrid example for others to learn by.*

*I recall vividly standing on the steps of the church after a very disturbing meeting with the group regarding the disbanding of it. The pastor exposed all my flaws and even imagined flaws he thought I had in front of the whole group of people I was trying so hard to fit in and be liked by.*

*One of the group leaders got up outraged at what he was doing and how "unchristian" it was. She stormed out of the room and left the church slamming the doors on the way.*

*I recall clearly there was more shock as she left the church. Was she actually able to slam such large heavy doors to begin with or what was actually taking place down there?*

*Moments later the sound of the town hall bells started ringing. You could feel the wonderment as if she or someone had gone over there to ring them to the heavens to make a statement of what type of injustice was being served in that town.*

So I stood there back on the steps of the front of the church confused…

*I didn't know where to go. I didn't know what to do.*

*I wasn't really even sure who I was anymore. Things were said to me, I was in a daze - I recall being invited to the Episcopal Church, by an older woman that also went there for an event coming up soon.*

*I stood on the steps, not even sure where I lived anymore. I literally did not know where to go or what direction to move in.*

*Things too extreme started to happen. Reactions from others - someone from the other side of the street sensing something strange was going on came over and he was told to go away.*

*The pastor stuck his head out an upper floor window and said what I can only recall as the strangest things ever. He was determined that those people on the steps with me had to get me off the church property and fast.*

*Within this memory, that is so strange, so surreal and so much of it I want to say is not real - it cannot be for real, it is too strange to be real. Yet from the bottom of my soul screams, it was real and this is what they did to you in their lack of ability of holding space for you or even being actual Christian themselves!*

*Sometime later, across the common from the church, a car pulled up and it seemed I was told and prodded to go to the car. I vaguely recall walking up to the car and feeling or thinking that it was my mother and stepfather. They were asking me what was going on and I just dazedly said I did not know. I think I may have even asked them who they were.*

*I was so confused I did not know who I was, where I was, where home was. I did not even know who these people in front of me were that wanted me to get in their car.*

*I assume I finally got in the car with them and at some point they took me back to my brothers where I was staying.*

*I have a memory of attending the Episcopal Church sometime after this. And again - I do not recall how I got home. There are parts of this memory that are so extreme that at this point, I do not feel comfortable telling, due to what they say about others.*

## I started to have a vision...

*What I will say is during the service, which I was told was a very sacred service that normally people were not allowed to attend unless they were an actual member of the church I started to have a vision.*

***I did the best I could to hold it back when I started to feel and see it happen.***

*I was sitting observing and listening to everything being said and yet I was seeing something energetically take place. It was as if the veil between worlds was separating and souls started screaming out to me from another realm.*

*I was losing my grip on the containment of my physical body. All these spirits flickered at me like flames. They tried to grab me for they wanted to come forth, back into the physical reality. It seemed like some strange sacrifice was being offered and I cried out things I cannot even recall. It seemed like all these spirits were trying to come forth through me.*

*I was terrified. It seemed these people in this church had no idea of the depths of what was going on and I cried out about the injustice.*

*As if instantaneously not only did I have all of the spirits I was seeing try to overtake me, I had everyone in the church turning and looking at me. People started screaming and I was shrieked at to leave. I cannot remember the things they said to me but it felt unloving and ungodly.*

*Now as I look back, I could question whether I was misunderstanding the realms I was seeing through and reacting from that perspective. Though, the thing that sticks with me to this day that makes me remember this memory as clearly as I do, is the fact that when I was outside, once again on the steps of a church, being asked to leave as I was literally thrown out of a church again.*

*On the other side of the big doors, on the floor inside the church, was the lady that invited me. She was crying over and over repeating the same things "But you are right, they do not see it… But you are right and they do not see it… But you are right and they do not see it."*

**Once again I found myself not sure where to go or where home was.**

*My family did not understand anything I was going through. All they comprehended was that Keith was having difficulties and losing his mind and going crazy. The things that I had dealt with all my life was beyond their scope of comprehension. They were not aware of the things I sensed or the reactions of others that I had to overcome.*

> My sister offered to pick me up to go for a visit. I didn't realize the visit she was referring to, was to take me to the mental ward at the local hospital. She brought me to "be checked out" and apparently she didn't tell anyone else in the family either, other than her husband, who drove us there

> **I sat there thinking, they should be admitted not me!**

This is a huge reminder to me of how much danger we can put ourselves in when we are being helped by people that do not know how to actually help us. We are in danger because their inability of comprehending turns into an added endangerment for us.

> I was brought into a quiet room. My sister and her husband spoke to me in a way that seemed to make me even more paranoid than I would have been if they would have just been quiet.

> It was decided, by whom I really am not sure, that I should stay there over night.

> When I look back that overnight stay it lasted at least three months. At nineteen I was in a "mental ward" of a hospital when most other nineteen year olds were out doing who knows what.

> Part of the time was a major blur since I was put on so much medication I just wanted to sleep my life away.

> I had no motivation. I really didn't understand why I was there. The pain I felt when I was around other people there was extreme. It just made me go deeper inside of the confusion of myself.

> I could overhear some of the talk about me. The nurses and staff discussed what my real problem must be. They couldn't seem to find a classification for me to fit within. They didn't want to send me back to my step brothers and no one else in the family was either able to take me or help me.

> **I spent from what I recall three months there due to this.**

> I recall telling them about some of my experiences. After a while it seemed like some of them knew that it was something much deeper and profound and REAL that I was going through. It was not the psychosis it might seem by someone not understanding the higher dimensions.

There is much I choose not to tell right now, of various experiences that happened during this time. There are things that tie in synchronicities that happened before and even after all of this which would explain much more in detail.

Why you might ask would I not add details that would show more realness to the story?

What I have for an answer is that I could go so deep into this chapter and the drama and trauma of the experience that it would take a volume of itself to do so. I choose to allow the reader the process of their own free will and introspect to decide what they believe and how they process their beliefs in a story that is full of outrageous plot lines as it is.

> My room was pretty much across from the nurses break room. I actually overheard much of what was going on in that ward from the nurses while I was in my room.

> At times, I also have an interesting ability of seeing what people are thinking when it is about me. Though, that information tends to fall into the category of "psychosis" in the hands of people not clearly using their senses.

> One of the strange things that I overheard was during a time at the end of my stay. There was an overflow of people self- admitting themselves into the hospital. The nurses commented how these people had no actual problems. According to what I overheard with my actual ears, the nurses suspected people were aware of "rumors of me" and wanted to be there due to the fact I was there.

Of course I realize how psychotic that does sound to state. This is one of the other things that happened that seems to feed into that thought process of being real.

**"It is The Hypnotic Spell and the Telepathic Control over and of the Human Race".**

> A lady was admitted for an overnight stay. Her husband was with her since they had driven from a far distance. They were on their way to a cancer clinic which was very different than a standard treatment facility. (Possibly he slept in his car that night I do not recall or know all those facts).

> Much was being said about the danger she was in, and how strong her faith was in her beliefs of becoming healthy without standard treatment.

> It was mentioned that what she was doing could actually be considered illegal. I suspected it had to do with the treatment she was going for or the treatment she was

refusing. She was being talked about as if some sort of celebrity, for what she was going through so courageously.

There was a group session organized for the morning. She was going to talk about her disease and what she was doing for treatment. Something about all this didn't seem to fit in properly to me.

I was feeling very strange as I walked into the room. I was noticing that something was going on that didn't either feel right, or that there was an illusion of some type starting to take place that seemed out of sorts for what was "supposed" to be taking place.

As I walked into the room the lady was whispering something directly in the face of the person in charge of the group circle. He then abruptly got up and left the room.

**Then the woman started talking fast to the group telling them they didn't have much time.**

She stated she was glad I had just walked in the room. She was aware I was sensing something taking place, and that I knew the truth as well, and I should sit with them and talk.

I started to get nervous. I was feeling like I didn't want to be part of all this - that it was getting "too real" for me to deal with again.

The lady was struggling with time to get her message out. She knew the group leader would be back within any moment. I was in the room but I was also aware of what was going on down the hall with the group leader. I was aware, but trying to run away from the space that was opening in front of me in this room I was in.

*The group leader ran back into the room all flustered and upset. He had just realized he was hypnotized to leave the room. The lady needed to have the space of the room alone without him there, to tell why she was really there.*

*He noticed me all agitated. He did not know what to do with a room of people that he literally had no control over.*

*The lady stood her ground. She worked to speak in a way that would wash over what he thought was going on. She tried to cover her tracks as to what was really happening. I left the room not knowing what to do.*

For some people reading this it just adds to the dilemma of what might be psychosis. What might be real? People need to learn to discern for their own. What is reality in this world full of illusions that we live within?

I have no desire to prove myself so to speak, with anything regarding this story or the book itself. I am telling the story of my life and some of the things I have experienced.

I have learned to discern from Ego, Judgment, Personality, Opinion and Learned Knowledge to get glimpses of the truth through the veils of illusion that society breeds upon us. Time has seemed to impregnate us within, what I would refer to as "The Hypnotic Spell and the Telepathic Control over and of the Human Race".

Utumei (oo – too – may)

The Essence of Enlightenment

Courtesy of: BePeaceNow.org

## On My Own for Real

**Out of a mental ward and into a foster home was a very strange place to be at nineteen.**

*It seemed there was no place for me to go. The hospital organized for me to move into a foster home to help my transition back into society.*

*A couple members of the hospital staff first brought me to a "group home" to see what I would think of that and how I would fit in there.*

*Upon entering the group home and getting a tour, I talked with the person that watched over the house. It was very apparent that I would not fit in there. A couple things said to me by the man earned him a sit down scolding from one of the men that came from the hospital with me. It seemed he was very excited for the possibility of me moving into the house with him, in fact improperly so.*

*So, it was decided I would move to a foster home with a rather large family. The mother of the house was nice and I got along well with her. She felt guilty for getting so much money for taking me in that she would take me out for lunch most every day. She got me out of the house so I could try to interact within society.*

> It was a good size house but filled with kids, their kids and more foster kids. There were way too many kids all in one place for me. I had to share a room with another foster boy that was probably sixteen or seventeen. Since I was on so much medication and basically a zombie I was pretty much a push over. I had to quietly deal with his own issues as he learned how to control me.
>
> I had such a hard time getting out of bed and really only wanted to sleep because of all the medication. I can remember being told that I had to get up, that I couldn't stay in bed all day. It was one of the hardest experiences I have ever had in struggling and forcing myself to get up each day when I felt like I had nothing to live for. Each day was torture being there.
>
> I didn't even have the consciousness to realize a lot of the issue was the amount and mixture of medication I was on at the time. The medication was literally repressing my state of being.
>
> I had no will power it seemed and I was totally disempowered from everything going on.

Once again there is much I will not go into regarding this period at this time and what happened. I will say it did not end well in several ways.

> I was back at my step brothers for a time and then at one of my sisters. Shortly after talking me into moving in with her and her husband she then decided it was time I needed to be on my own and suggested I find a place.

> I really had no money. I was feeling like once again the world was upending me and I was getting tossed on the street alone and unprotected. I moved into a disturbing rooming house and had to organize rides to work which was an ordeal in of itself.
>
> Life was a blur of trying to get to work. I had to survive while at work and then try to overcome my poor living situation of where I dreaded being.
>
> I had no actual friends and I didn't get to go places for quite some time.
>
> Life started to get better as I finally got off all my medications. I was determined that I would deal with my issues and that feeling pain was better than feeling nothing at all. No one was able or willing to help me. I had to learn to do it on my own.

(**Please note:** this is not a declaration to take yourself off medication. It is a statement that we all need to be part of our treatment plans. We need to make sure that those that are "managing our care" actually know what they are doing, and are qualified in doing so, with our best interests in mind.)

> I had a few friends at work, though that itself was drama. No one really held space for me other than what they either wanted from me or who they wanted and expected me to be for them.
>
> I was trying to discern my own space of being while feeling the judgment of others due to the fact I never really seemed to fit in anywhere I went.

Life as a very open highly empathic person is not easy if you do not have healthy boundaries – if you are not careful you become the people you are around energetically.

As shy and introverted as I was, two girls I knew invited me to go out with them to a little club in a restaurant in East Brookfield. I had a much larger older guy come up to me inches from my face and tell me I had to leave or he would kill me.

It was my first time in a club. But, it certainly wasn't the first time that someone got inches to my face and seriously threatened my life because they didn't like me, even though I had never said anything to them and they didn't even know me.

For a time I ended up living in a rooming house in Worcester, Massachusetts. There were times I did not know how I would even come up with the money to pay the rent each month. I recall the strange memory once of having enough money for food. So I went grocery shopping down the street and filled the refrigerator in my room to the point nothing else could fit into it. But then I don't even recall eating any of the food, I was so depressed.

By this point I had met someone that had introduced me to a local dance club. It was popular and safe to just go hang out and I started drinking. I couldn't drink anything stronger than beer or I would pretty much pass out. It didn't take very many beers to get me high and forgetting what I was feeling.

All I did was dance, dance and stand as a wall flower wishing someone would like me. I danced alone often not *caring about anything. All I could feel was the music pouring through me and the pain of life was pushed out of the way for the time.*

**I lost myself.**

**I lost the world in dancing.**

*I just wanted to feel loved. I just wanted to feel safe – I felt so very alone not realizing that there was a whole universe of angelic beings working to hold space for me.*

*There was a very dark period of time that passed for me. In between the nights of dancing then attempting to survive the days of losing jobs and struggling to make ends meet to pay the next week or month of rent and still be able to eat - there were days I did not eat.*

*There in that space, I barely existed. Months of not knowing if I would literally be on the streets homeless with no food – no actual friends of any depth or support and no family I could go to for help.*

*I can look back now and realize how often I was saved by disasters that struck around me. It could have been much worse for me. There were lessons apparently I had to learn and I had to learn them in the way I had to learn them.*

*In a way it was as if I was bidding my time and waiting. Dancing as painfully as it was through space to an appointed time when I could be reborn to whom I truly was.*

*I worked a short time at a fabric store and convenience stores.*

A convenience store is a strange place for a highly empathic person to find themselves. But somehow it was a lesson for me how to fit in and put on a mask, so to speak, and just work from my solar plexus. I was trying to assert an identity to come forward in the midst of everything.

Any job seemed better than my first job in this life — which was working at a chicken farm of all things. All day long wearing a mask over my mouth in an immensely smelly, sweltering hot, long barn in the summer picking eggs from thousands of chickens that were frightened and not happy to be disturbed.

At the convenience store in Worcester I was attacked in broad daylight by a group of kids that came in, jumped me and robbed things from the store.

Security for this particular chain of stores was to watch the sales clerks to make sure they were not stealing. They actually had a small room at the back of the store with a mirrored window. They would have security people sneak in from the back of the building and sit in there during whole shifts to watch who was working the store to see what they were doing. Yet they wouldn't come out and help the clerk if something went wrong in the store.

After I was jumped and finally got the door shut and locked to protect myself I called the store manager. I reported what happened and was yelled at because I told her I locked the doors.

She demanded that I open the doors. She told me not to call the police since she was a new manager she didn't want to deal with that issue and for me to just deal with it.

*She had no desire to come down to the store since it was Thanksgiving Day and it was her day off. She said she would fire me if I didn't do as she said - so I had better reopen the doors.*

*I hung up the phone, reopened the door and left. I honestly do not remember if I locked the door behind me – if the police had shown up, and found an unmanned store or what.*

*All I remember was that "IT WAS" Thanksgiving and I was thankful to still be alive. I was not going to put myself in that position again for someone that didn't care if I lived or died.*

*An ironic thing about the story is - that while the manager didn't want to leave home to help me, her home was within the same apartment complex I was sharing a room with someone at that time. So I went home to the same building she was in and didn't say a word to her.*

## Turning $50 into a Business and Hiding in Ambition

*In the past before I started losing myself in dancing, before I worked the odd jobs at the convenience store and learned to start standing up for myself I had worked at a local printing company in their warehouse. I stocked the shelves with the various papers and envelopes that would be needed in the press room to print on.*

*It seemed like an easy job compared to others I had in the past, with friendly people in the various departments that I would make casual friendships with. I was able to get a ride to work with someone else that lived nearby and I was getting out of the house more, if at least it was only to go to work.*

*My life while working for the printing company took some turns and as I stated before I moved into my sister's house. Shortly after this I was told that I had to move again. I then moved into a two room apartment above a local tavern. Nights were loud trying to fall asleep with live bands playing beneath me and not feeling comfortable there, not having anywhere else to go.*

*I worked to pay the weekly rent of $100.00 and to buy food to eat. As I look back I wonder how I even survived those days lost within myself with only a few people to actually talk to. I was running away, as fast as I could, from the things I was sensing all around me.*

*Life got much worse. Then I lost myself in nights out, thinking I might actually make friends.*

Fortunately in the end I did meet someone able to be a friend. His name was "Hal" and we rented an apartment together and helped each other survive.

**Somewhere within this time**

I befriended a lady that owned a flower shop when I started working at a convenience store around the corner from her shop.

It didn't take long till I started offering to help out while I was visiting. I was feeling as if I was part of something with others whom seemed to care about me. They took the time to listen as I developed the ability to express myself more.

I had gone from working at the printing company to a few other jobs. At some point, in all this, I decided since I had a working awareness of what was considered a "printing brokerage". Where a person would take orders from a catalog of business cards and social invitations then send the orders to the printer to actually print them. I could do this at my friends flower shop and possibly even bring in business for her at the same time.

I invested fifty dollars into a wedding stationary catalog and my first order from a customer was so large I made a little over three hundred dollars profit! I turned that around and bought more catalogs including some for business stationery. I had created a business basically from scratch.

*I reinvested all the money I could into advertising to promote the business. I put my attention into becoming "someone" in trying to find my sense of worth of self in having a business.*

**The Pen & Palette Line**

- Wedding Invitations
- Business & Social Announcements
- Letterheads
- Business Cards
- Promotional Advertising

Discounts When Ordering Wedding Flowers & Wedding Invitations Together

CALL KEITH
(508) 867-4464
Located at Tulips Flower Shop
West Brookfield

*Again, much happened that I would need the space of another whole book to explain. But within the first year my business was bringing in more customers on most days than my friends flower shop was. For some strange reason she really wasn't getting the extra brides coming in for wedding flowers as I had hoped when they got their invitations from me either.*

*My friend was taking more days off from the flower shop since I was there and able to watch the place for her. I started learning more about making flower arrangements at the same time as taking printing orders.*

*All the things going on started to create a separation between us. It was decided that I should move my ever expanding business somewhere else.*

*I sat at my desk wondering if the world was falling out from under me once again. Would I be able to pick it all up and move it somewhere else in that small town and still keep things going?*

*Leaving the store, to go home early for the night, I stopped at the convenience store next door. I was partly feeling like everything was falling apart. Yet at the same time feeling like this was a push from above that I needed. I sensed something or someone tell me it was going to be more than alright. I sensed I needed to buy a scratch lottery ticket to prove it.*

*I bought a one dollar scratch ticket and walked away winning a hundred dollars with a firmly implanted sense that it would work out and not to be bothered by the upcoming change.*

*I needed to move on. It seemed somehow life and the spirits around me were giving a push in a direction of movement. On the ride home I noticed there was a little two room office down the street that had a "for rent" sign. I went to look at it and found there was an apartment for rent next to the office as well.*

*I was living in Worcester Massachusetts at the time. My roommate Hal agreed to move to West Brookfield with me so that I could be closer to my business. We were able to rent the office space and the apartment together to save money.*

We cut a hole in the wall between the two spaces to connect them. We were very poor just making ends meet. My roommate at the time was the only person in my life that I felt safe with and that felt like family to me.

Hal worked very hard to help me build the business. He paid as many of the bills as he could, even bills relating to the business to help it survive.

I don't recall how long it was, but after a while – possibly a year my friend that owned the flower shop decided to close her store. I decided to buy her flower coolers and expand my printing business into a flower shop as well.

I really didn't know what I was doing regarding being a florist other than the few things I had learned while helping out.

I contacted someone that had been making and selling dried floral arrangements to see if she wanted to do design work at the shop. I asked if she would take care of that end of the business.

When she said she would I then purchased the floral coolers. I set up the companies we would take long distance orders from. I paid all fees involved. We were living month by month. The fact I had some extra money to do this at the time was really stretching things. I had faith and was determined to make something of the business. This was my outlet for hiding from the world and all I sensed within it. I could not lose that.

The day, that was to be the first day the flower shop would be selling flowers and the designer/limited partner would start, turned a path I wasn't expecting. When she walked in the door I knew before she even said anything. I was in shock from what I sensed. She didn't come in to help me with the flowers that just came in an hour before. She came in to tell me she was getting a divorce and wouldn't be able to do what we agreed upon. She apologized and gave me her dried floral arrangements in the store to make amends.

I was left realizing I needed to figure out how to be a florist on the spot and I did.

It wasn't easy. My entire attention and awareness went into the business. I was trying to make the right choices and grow a clientele base. While making things look wonderful on the outside, I felt hollow on the inside.

I didn't know how we would survive. It's a strange thing to own a business and handle money, investing it into products not knowing if you would sell the product or how fast you would.

If it was perishable, as flowers are, you wonder if the money would be going to waste. All the while knowing you really needed that money to buy groceries or pay rent. You know you have to go without, to try to 'pay success forward' in upcoming weeks and months.

I honestly am humbled when I think of my roommate Hal. How much he struggled through his own issues to work the hard jobs he had to work every day. Even while driving so far back and forth to get there - so that I could achieve what I was setting out to do in the country.

I am grateful for him being there for me. As far as I knew at that point in my life he was the only person that was truly there to protect me since I was so lost inside of myself. I often think he deserved a better roommate or friend than me back then. I was too busy running from my senses. I was trying to show the world I was not afraid of what was really going on all around me.

I wasn't truly there myself and so I wasn't able to be there for him or anyone else as well.

> *Much happened in those first years of going from someone that ran a business selling social and business stationery to expanding and running a business that as well was a full service florist and social consulting service.*

> *I was investing all my time and energy into my business at the same time as learning how to socialize while doing so. I may have been hiding the real me in the process or too lost to know who the real me was. It was a roller coaster of other people's emotions regardless.*

Much of what really happened I will not go into since I still live in that little town as I write this book. I know as it is when this does go to print; I may have to move away as it is.

> *Some years went by and we continually added to the offerings of the business to try to succeed and hence we became a gift shop.*

> *We sold antiques and even rented tuxedos. We offered live Christmas trees during the holidays. We developed a committed following of customers including people that would drive through several towns and go by several other florists just to get to us.*

*We were constantly told the business should be in Boston on Beacon Street. From what I could figure, since I had never been there, it must have been a very upscale place.*

*Surviving was still hard, more money would come in and bills would be higher. Then it looked like it might get easier. The building we were in was going up for auction. It looked like I was the only buyer interested. I was quietly loaned the ten percent that would be needed for the down payment. There were other tenants in the building their rents could help with the mortgage. All the figures we worked out made it seem like it would work in a very easy way.*

*As the time drew near, I heard from my realtor, that it was commented by others from the bank itself, that I was the only one that would be at the auction. No one else was showing interest.*

*Then a couple days before the auction the local bank told us they now would not accept the ten percent down but wanted more money. They already knew we couldn't come up with more money. I was confused as to why they would do this if we were the only ones interested in the building.*

*We were confused. From what we were told there was no one else interested. There was no way I could come up with the percentage they wanted. The day came and as I stood out in front of my business, not sure what was going to happen as they started the auction. A car drove into the parking lot and a man stepped out smoking a little cigar cigarette and made an offer of cash from what I heard and bought the building.*

*Within the week we received a letter from the lawyers of the new owners that gave us thirty days to vacate our apartment and the store itself.*

*Within those thirty days we received six of those same letters. On the side we were told as were the other people in the building, if we needed help moving stuff they had some "strong men" that could help us move in time.*

*Everything once again was up in the air. We started looking for another building that I could use the deposit on. I had no time to even consider if I was going to lose everything I had built up till this point. I felt like there was a black hole inside of me and that I would never get a chance to feel anything other than pain in my life.*

*My realtor showed me everything available in that small town even places off the beaten path yet nothing seemed to fit or made sense.*

*She kept trying to show me a little house that wasn't on the market but that she knew the owners would be willing to sell to us. It was just six houses away from where we were being thrown out of. Each time I drove by it, it just seemed too small.*

*The deadline loomed and finally with all other options lost I decided to look at that small house around the corner.*

*I walked in and realized right away this was the house. It was meant that I did not look at it before and waited till I didn't feel like I had options. I could then see how, the layout of this house was what we needed. In fact the house was much bigger than it looked from the outside. I kept exclaiming in shock as I was shown other rooms that there* was even more to the house, than we realized, while we were looking at it.

This house, which I still live in, has a strange ability to be there right in front of you yet at the same time not be showing everything it has to offer. Still to this day it has that rather mystical realm about it. As if it sits within a time portal of space just waiting for the discovery of all it contains.

> I made the best offer on the house I could and they accepted it. They offered to let us move in before we even officially signed the papers, telling us they knew what was going on at the other house. They knew we needed to get out of there as fast as we could, and even before the deadline if we could get our stuff out fast enough.
>
> I was cautioned that when it was found out that my business would move down the street and not actually fold that certain people would be very upset.
>
> Before we moved in, while I had the keys and it was mine to do what I wanted or was able with, I had a brief flash of what it would feel like to have the house just for us, not for the business but just for us to live like normal people.
>
> We needed to move the business in so that we could actually pay the mortgage. We needed to try to do it as fast as we could without really closing the day to day activities of the business in the process.
>
> That week, not only did we move our apartment and the entire store, I also was in the middle of organizing a wedding which was on the weekend.

*During that brief flash I looked through the windows of the front of the house onto the town common. I dreamed of a life of not being in fear and on the constant move to protect myself from others.*

*The business survived the drama and move. It flourished even more. I would walk down the street to the post office to get the mail and people would hit their car horns and wave at me.*

*I was that nice florist guy that they all thought they knew.*

*While quietly working in the building, doing my many chores and duties, I was actually lost within my consciousness. I seemed to feel safe or at least I made myself believe that to the best of my abilities.*

*I wasn't really interested in much of anything other than building the business. Walking down the street to get the mail lost its appeal. It actually bothered me when I would* be waving to ten cars or more hitting their horns with smiling people waving at me. I would realize in fact they actually didn't know me. It would trigger strange reactions within me of awareness of what I really did not have in life.

The ups and downs of business and life continued. At times I would try to have a social life. I was honestly miserably unhappy in life feeling lost and being dragged down by a sense of dread that had been with me my whole life.

**I would throw myself deeper into work so as not to pay attention to my senses, and the pain and what I feared from the future, that had not yet come, and the past that had still not lost its grip on me.**

One winter night I found myself at a bar in Worcester wearing my beat up old leather motorcycle jacket. Of course I didn't ride or own a motorcycle I was lucky to even have a car that was drivable. The jacket had its look and effect and all those months in the gym where paying off on helping me to feel good in my outer skin.

182

*I was getting a lot of attention that night and it seemed everyone wanted to be my friend, though it seems they had more on their minds.*

*I went home by myself but with a pocketful of phone numbers. The next week was a hard one as it was close to Christmas and we were in the middle of a bad snow storm. The furnace had just died with a whole store of flowering plants on the verge of freezing.*

*We were closed due to the storm and I wasn't sure what to do about the furnace. I was sitting in the living room debating to myself how can this situation be fixed. How can I afford to do it with all the expenses I had already accumulated buying product in hopes of selling during the holidays?*

*Once again what should have been starting to be a happy time started to feel like it might go downhill and cost me more money than I could afford. It seemed to feel like I was expecting "the next shoe to drop" as the phrase goes and something bad was always going to befall me.*

*I was pretty much starting to feel I had no hopes when the phone rang. On the phone was one of the guys that had given me his number the week before.*

*His name was Kevin. Out of all the guys I talked to that night he seemed the most sincere. I was too lost in pain to realize the connection. I was too lost in my consciousness to recall the memories from childhood of who I would meet later in life.*

*I was still repressing, as hard as I could, any of my psychic abilities that I did have as well as any memories regarding the fact it seemed I was a little bit different than what others showed themselves to be.*

*The connections of my consciousness would take some time to put the pieces together.*

*Kevin was at work, out towards Boston. He called stating that he was debating on leaving to go home due to the storm and asked what was going on with me.*

*I told him I had closed my business for the day because of the storm and that the furnace had gone out. I commented that I was deciding who to call to come fix it. He told me I shouldn't call anyone since they would charge a fortune to go on an emergency call during a snowstorm, the week of a holiday.*

*He asked what the furnace was or was not doing. I explained the best I could. He claimed it sounded like the motor had burnt out. He said that it actually was an easy fix. He just so happened to have an extra motor in his basement and he would go home and get it and be over as soon as he could get there.*

*I hung up the phone bewildered. Why would this guy drive thru a snow storm all the way from Boston and go home, pick up something that I didn't even understand what it was and bring it to my place? And then fix my furnace for me? And he actually had an extra one in his basement?*

*I wasn't really sure if he would show up, yet he did. Kevin fixed the furnace and in doing so saved all the plants in the store from freezing.*

**Kevin as a child**

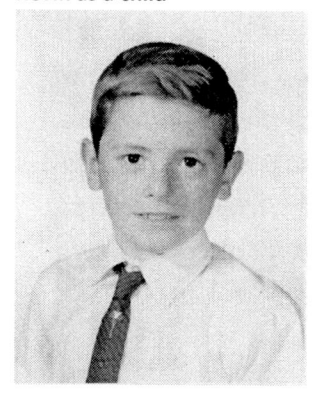

Little did I apparently comprehend at the time that Kevin was indeed the Kevin Moore I sensed I would meet several times as a small child. Then again he played a starring role when I was nineteen and I had one of the major visions of my current life.

I was so lost in trying to survive. I was hiding from trying to understand whatever it was that I was feeling in life.

Sorting it all out was the last thing on my mind and I wasn't present enough in the moment to comprehend the connections forming.

*Kevin was overcoming the death of his sister Tina from a few months previous. The few times he spoke of this I would get a sense of "Why do I know this already?" within me.*

*The first time I went to his house in South Grafton, Massachusetts, as we drove up I was confused why the house felt so familiar. I had already been there before.*

*On one side of my memories I had what seemed like recollections of a dream. I was remembering from my teenage years a dream of moving to a house in a series of towns and living with a new family that would protect me. I would remember how the house itself felt energetically, so much like the house in the dreams. Even to the point of how it was positioned on the street itself. It was within a series of towns made up of cardinal directions. That even related to the series of towns I myself had grown up in and the cardinal directions of the Brookfield's.*

*On the other side of what seemed like old memories was more recent within the space of my subconscious. It dealt with how I felt each time I would drive up to the house and walk to the side door. I would enter with the feeling of the kitchen and its state of being in the middle of what looked like a remodel. Even the room off to the kitchen seemed so familiar to me. When I entered it was as if I already knew the layout of the first floor of the house.*

In the future, when the walls would seemingly crash down all around me of my senses, I would unblock those memories. My perspectives would shift and I would understand how I was seeing into my future as a teenager. I had seen the options coming in how I would integrate my life with the lives of Kevin's family. The things I knew from childhood about them would all fit into place.

*I would come to remember the first day I went to that house. That house Kevin grew up and lived in for many years after his other family members moved from.*

*I would remember that in fact I went to that house once and visited a friend of Kevin's that lived there. I would remember that indeed Kevin was there that day. Even though energetically I felt his presence and his higher-self felt the presence of me it was not in the timing that we were supposed to meet. Forces would hold our physical meeting apart until later.*

*Though the heavens did open that afternoon as prophecies were quietly whispered, as if the energetic shift of two butterflies could be felt mating within the realms of the multidimensional universe we live within.*

### *That snowy winter day of the blizzard*

*Kevin came to my rescue as well as the rescue of my business at no charge with only the desire to be of help and be a friend.*

*With all his knowledge of plumbing, electrical and house repairs, not to mention a basement full of tools at his own house, he was a friend that was full of help during a time of hidden despair.*

*Much happened during those months, and even the following years, that I will not go into for the privacy of other people at this time. The business continued on with ups and downs as I was trying to still hold back my senses which were slowly but surely forcing their way back into my life. There is only so long we are able to live within illusion before the walls are penetrated.*

### *I don't want to be called Kevin any Moore -*

*Every time people would call me Kevin instead of Keith something would fire off in my mind. After a while I would start telling people when they apologized that I was used to being called Kevin, since childhood, and it was fine.*

*And then it kept happening more and more and I started to not be fine with it again. And one day after it kept happening I thought – Oh my god, why do people keep calling me Kevin! I have a right to be called Keith and I don't want to be called Kevin anymore and I am sick of it!*

*All the synapsis in my brain connected and cleared a memory from my childhood of thinking almost the exact thing!*

*I was standing in front of my friend Kevin. I was mad that everyone was calling me by his name and I didn't want to be called Kevin any more – I realized he was that Kevin Moore I had foreseen so many years ago.*

*Not only was he that Kevin Moore and not just any Kevin Moore that I might have happened to meet, but he was the same Kevin Moore with the sister named Tina that had a brain tumor while being pregnant with a child and passed away.*

*I would try repressing these facts for months due to the depths of them –*

*Though, the synchronicities of our lives would keep bringing back my memories of the connections between us and our families.*

*His mother was named Helen. My mother was named Helen.*

*My step sister Tina had passed away in a car accident when I was a child. She was holding a baby who died as well in her arms. Kevin's sister Tina who I would meet in visions, would also pass on from a brain tumor but was able to give birth to her child she was carrying first.*

*Kevin's middle name and his father's name is Daniel as was the name of my brother that died when he was nineteen.*

*And it goes on -*

*Dealing with others was getting harder to do. People would not communicate clearly and I would have to then sort out what was really going on. I struggled to keep up with everything going on around me.*

*It seemed all the customers wanted me to make their arrangements and take care of their needs. It was getting harder to allow others to share the load of work to give me space to breathe and be.*

*I would go through holiday seasons, like Christmas, working every day well into the evening and then wanting to only sleep on Christmas day.*

*I recall one particular holiday on Christmas Eve, at 8:00 p.m., as I was just finishing up and looking forward to go to bed and then possibly sleeping all day when the phone rang.*

*Of course I felt I had to take it and listened to someone begging me to do one more arrangement. They also wanted us to deliver it the next day on Christmas to someone they said was having a hard time.*

*They twisted the conversation of plight and concern for this person and how I had to do this one last arrangement. Even though I said we could do it after the holiday when we reopened.*

*I gave in, made the arrangement and had it delivered the next morning with the customer asking me to bill them.*

*The final sting of that last arrangement came when it was months later. The customer - someone I had actually known, had no desire to pay for the arrangement. She* claimed she was having problems paying her own bills. She stated I should be nice and let it go. She thought nothing more of me.

Dealing with customers and people in general was getting harder.

I would offer sales and special deals on flower arrangements when we got better prices from the wholesalers. Then some customers would complain later when I could not give the same sorts of deals at other times, even though they still were getting a good deal to begin with.

People would call and order flowers by name. Then they would call back to complain and try to blame us. For the fact that they didn't know what the flower was they asked for to begin with.

I learned not to design with the flower lisianthus no matter how beautiful it was since the average customer thought that the drooping stems were a sign that we gave them an arrangement of dead flowers.

It could be considered comical that the meaning of that particular flower is said that it communicates charisma and congeniality and if you send someone "Lisianthus" you are showing how much you appreciate their outgoing personality.

I got yelled at because some funeral directors emptied most of the water out of the containers so they wouldn't spill as they moved them, and then flowers wilted. A customer called right before closing on the night before Thanksgiving and demanding that I do a funeral arrangement for them.

*I stated that we didn't have enough flowers to do anything of quality. They stated they knew I performed magic with my arrangements and were confident that I could pull something together. Even though I claimed I could not.*

*They would not take no for an answer. They creatively let me know their position at the local church. The fact they ordered a lot of flowers from me meant I needed to do this one last arrangement.*

*I did take the order for the arrangement stating I offered that there was no guarantee they would be happy with it. Which of course they ignored my warning. I received a very angry phone call from them after the funeral due to the fact the arrangement did not look as beautiful as the others I had done. And yet they still did not comprehend the issues they had brought upon themselves. They declared they would not pay for the arrangement and instead would go elsewhere in the future.*

I of course learned years later, that I myself helped at times by co-creating some of those dramas by not setting my boundaries and sticking to them.

*Of course not all customers behaved this way. We did have many wonderful customers regardless to what could be considered insanity of others. Like people renting tuxedos for their wedding and then assuming that paying a three dollar insurance fee when renting meant that they could rent white tuxedos and then go play football in them, or not even return them to begin with.*

*I still can hear in my mind the groom I needed to call to ask when he was bringing his tuxedo back. It was already three weeks past and we hadn't heard anything from him. He yelled at me from the other end of the phone as he slammed it down "I will bring it back when I bring it back" of course he never brought it back.*

I could write a book all by itself of the all the outlandish things that happened (and possibly someday will) when dealing with the public in a retail setting and many of their confused sense of "The customer is always right" even when they are not!

**Becoming a business professional**

## A New Chapter Begins

*Then came the day I received the phone call from a woman that said she worked for a large shopping mall in Worcester Massachusetts "The Worcester Common Fashion Outlets". She was discussing with people that worked in her office that they wanted to bring a florist into the mall.*

*My name was mentioned as the person she should call. According to someone that told her this, I ran the most distinctive full service florist of the area.*

*I listened while fully aware I did not have the money to have a second store nor the time to try such a feat. Though, for some reason I actually made an appointment with her to go to the mall and see the space she wanted to offer me.*

*I walked into the empty store front and was astounded with the long row of windows I could be creative with, and the huge amount of space to sell stuff from.*

*Somehow I knew I was going to have a store there but did not comprehend how that was going to manifest into being.*

*She gave me her song and dance and offered a deal on the rent for a small percentage of our sales. It sounded too good to be true. I went home telling her I needed a few days to think about it. After telling Kevin all about the adventure, I knew it was going to actually happen, but I didn't understand how.*

*I was excited for all the possibilities of what looked like a much better future that might be forming ahead of us. Maybe this was the chance to really finally move ahead.*

*Before this new possibility came about Kevin's mother kept implying that possibly I just needed a better location for my business instead of being in such a small town with a limited customer base.*

Kevin's mother had great faith in god. She seemed to have a sense of knowing something I didn't often see. In conversations with her I always walked away suspecting much more happened than I realized. I seriously feel there were times she was directly communicating with someone within me other than me. I sensed she was fully aware of it and achieved a sense of strength at times when doing so.

*Kevin's mother offered money to help open the second store. Since the company Kevin was employed at folded he started actively taking part more in helping run the business.*

*I now had two stores and even more responsibilities while much less of a personal life. This seemed like the last push and attempt at trying to create a life for myself and its attempt to make something out of myself.*

I have since dealt with the fact that there is no need to try to make something out of ourselves for we already are. I was running deeper away from myself by doing more and working harder at doing anything other than being present within myself. I was getting closer to those final walls breaking down. I sensed so deep inside of myself that a huge change was coming. I wasn't sure how to deal with it.

**"Always a Bride never a Bridesmaid"**
**Keith being silly while setting up a wedding display in the store in the mall**

**The visions started coming back stronger and were harder to just push off and pretend that it wasn't happening.**

Memories from my childhood started pushing up from my subconscious wanting to be seen and heard and let loose. I was becoming aware that certain people I would meet were going to die and then they would shortly after.

It seemed, as if so many of those days at the mall, strangers would come in and interact with me in ways that were not normal. I would see, sense different realities happening all at once during those interactions.

Life was getting very multidimensional and I was feeling like I had a case of vertigo that would not let go. I was still using all my strength to ignore what was actually taking place. Yet on the other hand a part of me was doing very strange things which would get reactions from others that would stand out within the constructs of my mind and make it harder for me to dismiss.

It all seemed very peculiar and once again the uniqueness the strangeness, the quality of Keith, which makes him Keith, was coming forth in ways that could not be dismissed.

I would take little mini breaks and walk through the mall and try out little tests of sorts. I would decide something as random as taking a quiet walk and going within myself to hold just enough light about me to separate me energetically from the others walking around. I would hear hushed comments from people as, "Isn't that odd it is as if he is holding a candle".

*I would think something about someone and send the thought out to them with a push from within, but not look at the person directly, and they would turn and look at me and react.*

*There are other things I tried, that I wouldn't even dare at this point discuss. I know how strange it would sound to someone that doesn't know what we are actually capable of doing. Sometimes too much information for some people, not grounded within their bodies, is dangerous information.*

*I stood in line at the convenience store one night at that mall. I was literally being bored out of my mind waiting for my turn at the counter. I stood there with my mind blankly staring at the cover of 'The National Enquirer' which was on the rack a few feet away in front of me. I noticed a little story on Princess Diana and her new boyfriend.*

*The headline of the article rolled over and over in and on my blank mind, which as I said I was standing there literally bored out of my mind.*

*I saw in a flash the car accident. I saw bright flashes of light. I wasn't sure if I was seeing fire or what, but I saw Princess Diana and was witnessing her death and the death of her boyfriend the Sunday before it happened.*

***I walked from the store dumbfounded.***

*I think I literally was mumbling out loud to myself how horrible of a person I was to imagine something like that. Why would I do something like that and why am I such a crazed person to think of things like that? I beat myself up*

> within my mind, my spirit any and every way I could have during the walk back to my store that night.
>
> The next Sunday night I sat at my computer while I was at work. I was looking at the headlines of AOL, as it came on the screen that Princess Diana had just gotten into a tragic accident in Paris.
>
> My insides crumbled, my mind seemed to turn to slush. The same tears streamed down my face, as they are now typing this so many years later.
>
> I did not know what to think. It happened, though they were not saying she died yet. But I knew, though I couldn't think, I didn't want to think, I didn't know what to think and so I just cried. I went home and cried silently, the entire night, until morning came. I was so tired and numb I just moved onwards into an abyss.

During this time period we were trying to figure out how to move things ahead. How to acquire fewer responsibilities for me since I couldn't be in two stores at once and the other store in West Brookfield seemed to be not doing very well.

It seemed like only credit cards and an occasional check would come in and no one was spending any cash there anymore. I really wasn't sure what was happening since I was barely there and was leaving it to someone else to take care of.

> Kevin started to manage the store and depending on the day, I would say, mismanage the books for the business. He took on all the accounting from the other store as well.
>
> He started to notice some of the reasons there seemed to be no cash coming in from that store. He discovered why

*the return checks from the bills being paid out, seemed not to add up properly.*

*Then I got the phone call from my lawyer stating the bank wanted to know if I was keeping my house since I hadn't paid the mortgage in I think it was six months (or maybe it was eight months.)*

*Kevin suddenly realized that the other person that I thought was taking care of things for me was in fact, not. Things were much worse financially than we had thought at this point.*

*I was feeling more lost. I was lost in the load of work seven days a week, from early morning to the evening, because we had to keep the store open all the hours of the mall. Everything was getting out of hand.*

*I had an idea. What if we created a contest and gave away the house and the business in West Brookfield! I had seen things on TV and articles in the newspaper about things like this going on around the world. So I created "Sharing the Dream" a contest to WIN A HOUSE and a Flower Shop! All you needed to do was write an article about why you should win and pay an entry fee.*

*For a small entry fee, a chance to give your best reasoning for wanting to take part in this dream and expand it for yourself, anyone could enter with a limit of entries to keep the contest fair. I only wanted to make enough to pay off the mortgage and move on with my life.*

When I look back the contest was a blur. I was on the local news, in articles in the newspapers and even one in a national florist magazine. My visions were causing more disruptions and I was on sensory overload. I just wanted out, in fact I wanted out of everything going on at this point but I didn't know how to achieve that.

> I had an idea to send a very expensive flower arrangement to 'The Rosie Show' to Rosie O'Donnell. She had one of the biggest talk shows on daytime TV and was the "Queen of Nice" and gave away all sorts of stuff on her show. If we could get her to notice my contest maybe she would have me on her show to promote it, which would guarantee its success.
>
> The flower arrangement was ordered from a florist that I found in my book for calling orders out of state. It was to only have the web address of the contest on it, nothing else in hopes she would look deeper into what we were up to.

What happened next, is actually something, I would repress deep into my subconscious for many years later.

I ask, that you remember, as I tell this story and even possibly lightly imagine yourself, as me, for a moment in trying to find sanity within your senses that just seem to be going on overload. Having visions and then seeing them take place, dealing with things that are so strange and psychotic sounding, YET REAL, that I can't even go into them here due to the depths of them.

> Many years later I would deal with un-repressing the fact that Rosie O'Donnell did in fact get that flower arrangement. (Though as I hung up the phone from the florist after I placed the order, I wondered if they would even send it and how would I know if they didn't) Rosie O'Donnell actually came into my store and introduced herself and tried to ask me about the contest.

*I actually was on my way trying to leave the store to go for a walk in the mall. She walked in with her girlfriend and we met face to face in the middle of the store as we both walked up to each other.*

*She introduced herself as Rosie O'Donnell and as I looked at her thinking of the woman I often saw on 'The Rosie Show' I did not see "Rosie" and for whatever reason that came over me, in my already fragile state of consciousness, I replied blankly, "You are not Rosie O'Donnell, I know what she looks like and you look nothing like her!"*

*I was looking at a woman with no makeup on, her hair not done up, and in very casual clothes and could not fathom why this woman was saying this to me.*

*Still being gracious she offered her wallet and her license to prove to me she was who she said she was. I looked at her license and laughed and said - it says: "Rose Marie O'Donnell" see I blurted "I told you that you were not Rosie O'Donnell!"*

*Rosie tried to explain that her legal name was Rose Marie not Rosie, yet I would not hear of it and refused to listen to what she was telling me.*

*Partly confused and partially embarrassed for my own behavior I did not and would not listen. My states of consciousness felt like they were ripping apart from within me as if I was being attacked by a hurricane within the constructs of my own mind.*

*Her girlfriend mumbled something to her about, "let's get out of here I don't know why you put up with people like you do all the time".*

> Rosie, obviously confused by me, was still trying to understand what was going on and why I was behaving the way I was and I would not have anything to do with her.
>
> She started to motion to the large sign hanging behind the counter on the wall that declared "Sharing the Dream Contest!" I just walked away from her, confused as to who she was, while being adamant I was right and she was wrong. Part of me deep down was feeling like I was making a huge fool of myself. I felt lost in what was even going on all around me.
>
> All I knew was I wanted to get away from what was going on and walked away from her.

I would later realize that as I walked away from her I was forming another state of ego as I repressed the confused one I didn't want to deal with. It would take me years to not only un-repress that state of ego, but then many more I would create in dealing with all the things going on around me that I couldn't handle at that time.

I would learn I had been repressing things most of my life, creating energetic blocks within my states of consciousness that would someday want and need to be released no matter what was holding them back. I would learn through various therapies, as well as my own training in clinical hypnotherapy, what states of ego actually are and how to work with them to become clear within our consciousness.

I would also realize how wonderful and compassionate Rosie O'Donnell actually was in how she handled herself in that situation.

One of the things that helped me pull this memory out from my subconscious to deal with it, was the day I was watching 'The View' and Rosie was on talking about how people in the past did not recognize her when she was out in public without all the pancake makeup on.

She went on to tell how she had actually gone into malls, had to show her license to prove who she was and sometimes even still, she added, people do not believe her. I sat there in shock or better yet, I sat there recovering from shock to the fact she was actually talking about me. I wanted to call out to her on the TV screen in front of me and apologize for how foolish I behaved.

It took some years after that to understand it probably was not meant that I was to appear on her show. If I had, the attention would have most likely made the contest a success and I would have given away the home, I currently live in, and run a Holistic Center from.

If the contest succeeded, yes, I would have paid off bills. Yet only god knows where I may have ended in that battle that was going on for the attention of my soul.

As it turned out when all the walls came crushing down I needed that house to go back to. I basically became a recluse once again for several years to heal and regroup my senses and understand everything that had been going on my entire life.

I spent several years away from others. I was lost in the yard creating gardens out of every square inch of the property, finding the way back to my senses in the soil and flowers.

I needed to learn how to retake control of my life with working with my processes and my awareness instead of hiding and repressing from the things I sensed all around me.

The contest did not succeed, thank god. We gave back the entry fees and the whole process cost me more money than I could afford already. I closed the store in the mall and then would, not long later, close the store within my home in West Brookfield since I could no longer work.

**Front Gardens at 'The Holistic Center', West Brookfield, Massachusetts**

## Reiki is Love

When I look back within this current life of mine and ponder at what time I first learned of Reiki, I cannot honestly say that I know when it was.

Within all the visions, I had growing up as a child, certain things seemed blocked from my awareness for some reason.

It is as if all the light, that I now know and have in my life, was too bright to be clearly seen or distinguished through all the fear I was experiencing from my own misunderstanding of the disconnection of my spirit upon entering into the $3^{rd}$ dimensional realm that we believe we exist within. From all the energies of fear and hatred I felt from others, I was open like a sponge taking on and reacting to and from all the energies around me.

One of the things I have been saying for the last few years, with my Reiki students, is that if in the end I teach or attempt to facilitate teaching anything it is of "discernment". For Reiki teaches itself to people in the mystery of connecting to light in the way that it does.

Yes, a trained guide in the physical realm is needed, to help coach and show from experience things that make the path safer for the person learning. The actual energetic attunements of Reiki are best when they are in person by someone trained in the alignment of mind, body, and spirit energies.

I will not try to teach Reiki within these pages, for this book would need to be dedicated to that alone. I do plan on actually writing one of my next books for that purpose of being a Reiki guide book. Though, with all that said, I will offer certain information so that the reader that is not familiar with Reiki will gain a better understanding of where I am coming from within these matters as I discuss them.

I do realize as well that some people reading this book, that believe they are trained in Reiki, may realize in fact that this book teaches them more about Reiki than they have learned within the classes they have taken. I point this out for awareness and discernment of what is Reiki and the many misconceptions of it.

The term Reiki (pronounced Ray-Key) originated from the Japanese language and the word itself is made of two kanji (Japanese symbols) Rei and Ki which, when translated into English, can mean: Universally guided life/spirit force/consciousness.

The term is associated with a Japanese man by the name of Mikao Usui who is often referred to as "Doctor." Even though he was not an official licensed medical doctor, that one would consider within the western culture. He served in a healing service for others and was thus given that title out of respect and gratitude of his service.

It is said that Mikao Usui in 1922 had a spiritual awakening on Mount Kurama in Japan and received knowledge of a series of techniques which include the use of "symbols" that allows universally guided spirit/life consciousness to flow more easily through energetic obstructions to clear things such as disease and discontent and helps to align energy fields into balance.

Within the spiritual awakening of Mikao Usui he received an "attunement" of his energy fields by spirit. Those that are properly trained within this system of "energy work" are taught how to work with spirit to offer these energetic spiritual attunements to others, within structured levels of trainings, as well as general healing sessions where a person can receive a "treatment" of Reiki to help balance their energy fields and their connection to spirit.

Reiki is a very sacred subject to me. There are many levels and depths to it that I believe are helpful to be comprehended. Though a person does not need to understand or do anything to receive a treatment session of Reiki, other than to just allow their "free will" the experience.

Reiki can do no harm and does not go against a person's free will. With that said, if a person is using their free will to be unhappy and they are creating disease of their energy fields then they need to work with their free will to allow the energy to balance and Reiki can assist with this process.

The symbols that are used within Reiki training/teaching and sessions have very sacred meanings and use to me. I believe they are worthy of utmost respect to keep our connection to them pure. For this reason, I feel as do many others, that it is ill advised to show or discuss too much about them publically. They work best with a person that does not have other energetic attachments to the symbols other than their pure use of intent.

Because of this I caution people to not search online on computers about Reiki in case they may come across websites that do not respect these energetic concerns. One of the best websites that goes into detail about Reiki but holds a healthy boundary is www.Reiki.org

I feel it is fine to discuss the casual names of the Reiki Symbols and explain what they mean and how they can be used when it is proper. I do not discuss or say the actual names of the symbols for reasons of respect and sacredness of intent. This does not mean the symbols themselves are sacred, but rather that it is a sacred intent around the symbols that is the concern.

The casual names of the symbols that I will discuss here are the: Power Symbol, Mental/Emotional Symbol, The Distance Symbol and the "Master" symbol.

I will not go too deep into this but to briefly state that the -

**Power Symbol** can be used to access and allow the Reiki to start to flow when a person wants to begin to work with the energy. It also allows one to create and hold boundaries of space for working and living within and can be used to help "seal" a person's energy fields/aura so that all their energy does not leak out of them or that they do not like a sponge, taking on all the energy around them. It allows for the person's energy to be contained within the dimensions they need.

**The Mental/Emotional Symbol** which again is the casual name for this symbol used for reference is a symbol that allows the left and right hemispheres of the brain and energetic body to come into balance and align to the core of the person.

**The Distance Symbol** is used to be able to allow the energy not only to move through time and space to someone not in the same physical space as you, but also to a space within the past or future of "time".

I have allowed Reiki to flow backwards in time to spaces of my childhood within my energetic spirit to heal old wounds and traumas that occurred back then. I literally have felt those traumas lift and heal and while doing so. The fractured state of ego or portion of me rises up through the depths and levels of my being and integrates, aligns, and heals with my present state of being.

Due to the fact Reiki does not control the free will of others Reiki cannot be used to alter events in time or change history. It can heal the diseases and traumas that where caused in those experiences for those willing to allow it to do so.

**The "Master" Symbol** is for helping with the state of "being" of a person much like creating a state of "meditativeness of their being" working with it. It also is used with the other symbols in various ways within the attunement process when a person is being initiated into a level or degree of Reiki.

In working with spirit and Reiki, the one thing I do the most is to learn how to discern. Discernment of what is my energy versus another's energy or even the energy, of a spirit not in physical form. Discernment of pure energy devoid of attachments of fears and agendas, creating a reactionary realm that can take away the free will of a person through loss and confusion of their dis-attachment from their own spirit.

Understanding and learning to separate and discern the elements and levels of depths of **Ego, Judgment, Opinion, Personality, and Learned Knowledge** to actually hold clear space of being for our spirit of consciousness, is crucial to living and awaking ones spirit of being.

**Allowing our egos** to heal and become healthy. Having their place within the balance of our beings not overtaking us or others, but as well not misbelieving we are supposed to destroy our ego to become "better beings" as some will try to falsely mislead you by their own misunderstandings of their ego.

**Allowing judgment** to fall away, and in its place allowing the grace of discernment to take its place within us, will hold space while creating healthy boundaries to work within. To allow the energies to balance, as they are able, yet still be flexible for new growth to come through to us.

**Allowing opinion** the healing it requires to let go of its reactive needs of perspective claims of opinions with the blessings of acceptance and forgiveness for all that is, and is not. To see that all is much bigger than we comprehend within the 3$^{rd}$ dimensional space of our physicality.

**Allowing personality** to return to its place, behind the proverbial horse and wagon so that we do not become lost and trip over illusions of ourselves. So we can awaken to whom that we really are instead of being distracted and disillusioned from spirit by the clouds and dust of our actions.

**Allowing learned knowledge** the space to possibly be proven to be false or greater than we have assumed or comprehended. As well as holding space to allow more knowledge to come forth since one cannot take on more if we or others have built walls of knowledge around us, limiting our view of the space of what is.

Understanding how we ourselves fit in within these concepts of our actions and reactions of what we call and consider ourselves to be, is crucial to unleash the power of what we are capable of doing in this lifetime or any lifetime.

**Knowledge of these things will allow us as a race of people to finally come together and live in peace amongst ourselves.**

Comprehension of these things will allow us to finally realize once again, that we are actually spiritual beings only showing forth as human beings, for the experiences that can be in the physical realm of existence.

I often tell students that I attempt to facilitate the teaching of Reiki for Reiki unfolds its teachings, itself, as a person allows with their free will to process the experience through the dimensions of their beings.

It is often said, as well, that no one can really teach us anything, that it is up to us to allow our minds to work or not work in that process.

When I attempt to hold space, for teaching, I believe it is the space between me and the other person or the group of people, that really is doing the teaching and within that space is spirit.

It is not always easy to "teach" in this manner for if a person is not able or willing to come forward to be present in a situation like this, there is much they miss during the experience.

If a person is not used to this form of teaching as well - if they are normally the type that charges in with their ego, judgment, opinion, personality or learned knowledge, it sometimes can be challenging to get them to get out of the space in front and between us so that the space itself can be the lead and teacher.

As I sit within circles of this nature, observing what is going on in front and around me, learning each time to discern what I am feeling and experiencing, I am often surprised by the depths of the things I witness, I feel the need not to discuss or mention due to knowing it would cause more disruption within the energetic fields of the space as it is.

> *I have had to learn to discern the difference from what a person thought innocently was their spirit guide helping*

> them, when in fact it seemed more like either a spirit attachment with a very large agenda or their own displaced ego coming forth to take control, not only of themselves but anyone around it was able to grasp onto, to use for its agenda of claiming self-worth of doing as opposed to being.

After working with the technique and energies of Reiki, and when I look back at my childhood, I have realized that spirit had been teaching me things about Reiki for a very long time. I have been learning to discern ever since I was born and even have memories within the womb and then within the playpen of discerning what was going on.

> Spirit came to me as a child during a time of very dark and disturbing nightmares, which seemed more like visions of past and possible future wars.
>
> I would go to bed and suddenly feel like I was transported into a battlefield seeing and experiencing all the pain. I would awake screaming and too frightened to go back to sleep.
>
> During this time spirit came and showed me how to work with what I would later realize to be "The Reiki Power Symbol" to help give myself a boundary from those visions and space so that I could rest and sleep.
>
> I have fleeting memories of comments of other people "about what I would do later in life" and even recall comments that were negative, by those that were fear based, as to what I would be involved in later in life.
>
> Often when I overheard or sensed an adversarial nature of these people regarding my future life and my sensory abilities, there was a part of me that quietly noted how

*while they were busy judging me then, for something they apparently sensed or where told I would do or be in my future, they themselves seemed to be doing that "black magic" something that they cursed about me.*

*I can recall, vividly, times I just wanted to speak out if I could and say something of the sort, "well, explain to me what I am supposed to do with my senses instead of judging me for things I have not yet done, that you yourself are sensing I am going to do, and thus are possibly creating some of the situations of my senses you claim I should not have."*

*"Yet you yourself seem to be doing it with "black magic" while all along, all I am looking for, is love and protection because I sense the fear of you."*

My mentor, friend and the man I consider like a dad to me, John Livingston once said to me:

**"They are blaming you for the fact they themselves have not done their own work."**

Working with Reiki has allowed me to overcome all fears that I have had. Reiki allows me to raise my consciousness to higher dimensions of being and realize more of that which I really am.

I now realize the reflection of judgment I sometimes see within others eyes and the opinionated telepathic thoughts of others are not who I am. No longer am I lost in the "see" of others.

I have trained in the Usui technique of Reiki as well as one with more "Tibetan" influence of symbols and also have gone onto further training with William Rand of "The International Center for Reiki Training" and learned Karuna® Reiki which has many more symbols to work with. I have and continue to study with William Rand and also with Laurelle Shanti Gaia and Michael Baird.

I firmly believe that being open to learning from new teachers, which are appropriate for you, is important in life as well in Reiki training.

I believe in the term that the Japanese originally used instead of Reiki "Master", they use "Shinpiden", which means mystery teaching – for it is an ever unfolding mystery to hold space for revealing its treasures.

I also have been working with what I would call an "Egyptian" style of Reiki, which spirit itself has been teaching me and seems to relate to what appears to be past life information as an Egyptian. During this process of learning and unfolding this knowledge, it appears as if symbols and knowledge itself is shown to be what would have been considered Egyptian deities.

If you have never experienced a Reiki session then the only way to really understand what Reiki is, is to have a Reiki session with someone you feel comfortable with.

There are many ways to have a session and it can be done in person or from a distance. I suggest, for a first time session, it is best to have it in person so that you can discuss your experiences with the person, after the session if you wish and have a more personal guide of the experience in this manner.

You can sit up or lay down on a therapy table. Laying down tends to allow more of a relaxing experience and since we are working with energy fields a person's clothes stay on and in fact you can even be covered by a blanket since the energy can transmit right through the material fields.

Often people will start sessions in various ways. Either offering hands lightly on the body or hold their hands at a distance and allow the energy to flow. They might start at the head of the person and work down the body or start at the feet and work up. Sometimes they target specific areas without going in one direction or another. Much more is going on than can be seen in the physical realm with the physical eyes.

I weave Reiki into many of the therapies I offer and work to just breathe Reiki. Some of my favorite sessions are with clients that as I would say "work with their processes" to a great degree. Both I and client reach enormous heights within the higher dimensions during the session and have visionary experiences that are ineffable to the uninitiated lay person.

Mom, Hal, Keith, Kevin – Christmas Gathering

# Holding Space during the Passing on of Others

My beloved dog "Buddie" taught me much on passing over to the other side. Buddie was a Lhasa Apso, that I found at a local pound, on a search for a little dog to take home and rescue.

*We walked into the pound looking at all the dogs determinedly deciding to get a small dog but one that would be the most in need, not the cutest or most friendly, but the one that needed to come home with us.*

*I actually walked in hoping it would be a Lhasa Apso (or maybe it was that I already knew that it would be).*

*I saw the little guy and noted that he was pretty filthy and didn't seem all that friendly at first. Though I kept looking, determined that I would see all the dogs before I made my decision, I then went back to him realizing indeed he was the one.*

*Well, actually there were two – brothers we were told, and in fact, the girl at the rescue league seemed surprised we wanted to take either of them.*

*We were told that since no one wanted them and they did not seem to have control over their body functions they were scheduled to be put down the next day. We took both home, as dirty and covered in their urine and feces as they were, offering them as much love as we could.*

*It became apparent at home, that one of the dogs was the one with the issue of no control over his bowels, and the other one was just afraid and cuddled with him so it seemed like he had the issue as well.*

*I was later told by psychics that "Buddie" was an empathic dog and would try taking on the issues of others on him. He would try clearing them of their problems and I assume this is what he was attempting to do for his brother.*

*Sadly we had to let Buddies brother go back to the pound to be put to sleep since we could not handle the stress of the situation and needed to concentrate on helping Buddie.*

When I look back at this experience I wish I was able to hold space for Buddies brother as well – even to just make a pen outside for him and allow him to be and live out his last days as best he could.

I was in the process of getting over a major energetic shift that was preparing me to awaken to my awareness once again. He needed more help than we could offer. The issues regarding his particular conditions were beyond medical help to begin with. Even though he was not able to be helped, I blamed myself anyhow. The best that could be done was to help him from suffering.

*I was so lucid from all the visions I was currently having. I had just gotten out of staying in the hospital for three days.*

*I had not yet officially discovered Reiki, and I was in the midst of just starting my long journey of several years being a recluse again while working in my gardens trying to find my own spiritual center.*

*It took a few days for Buddie to actually come to us. He hid in the corners of the rooms and then over time started to become friendlier. Then, the medication I was on would make me feel like a zombie. It was as if I was getting even more lucid and wasn't sure what was real around me. Was I really seeing spirits and hearing voices? Or was it all in my mind? Was I indeed crazy? As I was fully aware, some thought of me.*

*Buddie was learning not to be afraid and started coming to me. I was battling being afraid and at times would need to distance myself from him in confusion.*

*Buddie and I went through a period of both being in fear, needing love and finding our way out of a very confusing time together.*

*I realized that the medication I was on was not healthy for me. It would either make me tired and not able to do anything or it would heighten my senses even more and make me delusional. I decided to stop taking the medication and deal with what I was experiencing.*

**This in no way is medical advice or recommendation regarding medication – each person needs to discuss their own particular needs regarding medications with the proper doctor for themselves that empowers them to health.**

> I spent over six years working in my gardens. Taking out all the grass in the yard I built garden bed, after garden bed. Connecting to the earth, grounding myself within life, to see what was actually true beyond the veil of illusions. I somehow found Reiki again and started to work with it daily.

Ten years after rescuing Buddie, we had to come to a sad realization that we would have to help him pass over. I will not go into the details other than to tell the story of his passing.

> It was a hard decision but it appeared to be the right one to help him from his pain. During the process I was afraid of what I would feel after. I knew that I couldn't show fear or pain. I realized I needed to hold space for him of love to allow him to pass upwards within the higher dimensional realms without witnessing my pain for him.
>
> I wondered if dogs went to heaven. Who would be waiting for him as he passed? I tried to block all of those thoughts and emotions from my consciousness and put my hands near his head. I offered to let the energy of Reiki flow thru him to assist in passing.
>
> All of a sudden I was overwhelmed by a huge but small force of energy. It burst from the top of his head and entered straight into my heart.
>
> It was the most love I can ever recall feeling. I stood in shock. I was dazed that he just passed and went straight into my heart. I saw within and to the right of me a male spirit in robes with open arms. It was as if the energy of Buddies spirit was taken within his arms and ascended

*upwards. It was then that I realized that never again can someone tell me that dogs do not go to heaven.*

## "The Tibetan Book of Living and Dying"

The Tibetan Book of Living and Dying is something I think everyone should consider reading. I think it should be required reading if you work in a field that deals with the passing over of others. It can teach you to understand what is needed in holding space for others during such a precious and sacred time we all experience.

I was fortunate to have read it before Buddies passing. It helped me during the passing of a friend that I will discuss next.

This story is one that I hesitated on telling due to the fact it might upset some people. Though, I feel it must be told. For purposes of privacy and non-judgment, I will not say names and will change things slightly without lying or adding to the story.

> *Working with Reiki I am often asked to help people during their time of passing. I consider this a sacred privilege when asked.*
>
> *I had a very dear client that was given, by their doctor, a set amount of time to live due to the fact he had a terminal illness.*
>
> *I feel it is irresponsible of doctors ethically and medically, to tell a person such a direct time frame of death. In doing so it takes away from their patients minds and spirit any chance of miracle or even the empowerment of when they will pass.*

*My client seemed determined that the six months was a death sentence. It was a death sentence to be fulfilled on that dates arrival. My Reiki sessions with him were a very painful experience for me to witness and hold space for.*

*I was asked if I could help during the passing to make it easier. I planned to be present and help if I could for that.*

*The issues within the passing seemed to become evident to me right away. Even though I knew that the clients other half had once read "The Tibetan Book of Living and Dying" it became apparent that they would not be able to hold space for their loved one in the way that was needed for them.*

*The whole passing turned into a battle of anger over the fact the person was dying. The anger was being taken out on the dying person themselves.*

*I tried to suggest counseling to overcome the issues that would and were coming up. Gently with love I would hold space for the client as well as their relationship knowing that the relationship between those two people needed to heal for the passing. But no matter what I would say the clients other half energetically let me know not to go there and that they would not listen to me.*

*This death was all about them and how it was affecting them. It really was not about the person that was dying.*

*I witnessed in horror, as time went on, how when we do not hold space for others, whether during their deaths or as part of their lives what happens to the people involved.*

*As happens often, during death, the families of these people all played various parts and roles within the drama as it unfolded. Each person's own issues came to play into how much space they could or could not hold for the person passing on.*

*I received a phone call stating that it was most likely the last day for the client. If I could come, I should, I was told.*

*My friend Kevin brought me to their house knowing that it would be a hard experience for me to witness. He knew even though I was asked to be part of helping the passing I was not being given the space myself to do so. Each time I tried to do what was really needed I was pushed back. Therefore I could just hold the space that was allowed for me to hold and pray that the lessons would be learned in the end.*

*Another person I know was asked to help out as well since they had experience in Hospice. Even though he originally said he would be there, as time went on he realized that he should stay away from the unfolding drama and just allow the official Hospice workers do their jobs as best they could.*

*I had a vision as I walked up to the steps leading to their house. I turned and said to Kevin that I was sensing and hearing that this would indeed be the last time I entered this house while the person was alive. The next time that I entered the house it would be for their wake.*

*I stood there, half in tears, blocking Kevin from entering the house. I demanded for him to explain to me why they would be waking the client in the house. I knew that indeed that was not the plans and I was confused. I did not like* everything I was feeling. Kevin, in his good catholic upbringing, told me he didn't understand but that we needed to go inside. I knew what I saw was true, yet I didn't comprehend the perspective at the time.

The house was full of people. There was an energetic battle raging, of those not knowing what to do or how to react, to those immersed in how this was all affecting them. Lost within all this was the fact it truly was about a person in the other room working out their last days of processing the circumstances of their life and the relationships within it.

**I sat and gently offered Reiki.**

I decided I would put my hand on top of his head and see if spirit would allow him to pass and I was shocked with the response I received.

It was as if I was energetically slapped off of him. He needed the time to work out what was going on with his other half and the key to "their" passing relied on that.

I held space of Reiki around him, allowing him to feel the love of the Reiki, in hopes he would not feel all the other discord going on within the house.

I made a few comments to the person's loved ones to gently help him learn how to work through what was really going on. I told them that it was them actually not allowing the passing to take place. I went on and explained that, the dying person needed to resolve a conflict with them that they would not address.

I received looks of reactive anger, then some understanding, as to what was going on. But they were not *ready to resolve the conflict with their loved one and the loved one was not willing to die. He was holding on because of this.*

*In the midst of all of this there was a battle between certain ones of their family. How much morphine should be given to the dying person was disputed since it was feared that in giving the morphine they were just killing him.*

*From what I could see it seemed they did not have a better alternative. They did not appear to know how to properly administer the drug to begin with, in the reactionary states they were unfolding for themselves, in the drama they created between each other.*

*I sat holding space of Reiki as one of their family members came up and asked the dying person if they would like their help. The man lying there in the bed nodded in agreement and said yes and then tried to get up.*

*I seriously do not think he realized what was meant by "help" I myself was not sure what was meant by that. I knew from what I sensed with the Reiki that the person was not ready to pass and had more energy in him to be able to pass at that time.*

*Kevin came up to me and mentioned that he had to leave. It was very early in the morning and he had to be at work in a couple hours. Did I want to stay, or go with him?*

*Of course I did not want to stay, alone, in that environment without the protection of Kevin. Since all the signs I saw did not indicate that the man would pass naturally before the next day I could come back again.*

Though, I was still confused as I left the house as to what I sensed when I first walked in.

A couple hours later I was lying in bed asleep, yet I was very aware. I was feeling an energetic battle back at their house. I was hearing things as to if I should get up and go back over there. I was seeing/feeling the whole drama play out within my consciousness and even in what seemed my body.

As I lay in my own bed it felt as if there was a huge struggle going on. The dying person was raging with energy and trying to get up, out of bed, yet he was being forced back into bed.

He did not want to die and he did not want to stay in that bed. His free will seemed as if it was being taken away from him by people that would not allow true space being held for him in his times of need. They did not know how.

I stayed in bed confused, but aware that I was more there with him than not. I would truly not be listened to and what I could offer would not be respected if I did go there. I was holding space from where I was already. Even though I was half asleep I held the space of my being for him.

I received a phone call shortly afterwards that the passing had taken place. I was told that it was like a horrible battle that the person fought back to their death.

Kevin decided to go into work late and brought me back to the house. I walked up the steps recalling vividly the visions from hours earlier of this being the time of walking into the house as if it was a wake.

I have to say the shock of what those visions meant when I walked in the house and saw with the proper perspective how clear they really were is telling.

*Though I will not tell what I saw at this time.*

*When their family members heard that I had visions of the passing from my own bed, I was told something by one of them a few days later. I had not seen this in my visions or if I did, it was too painful to comprehend at that time.*

*I was told, that since there was a squabble about how much morphine and the best way to administer it for the person, was a major issue. Because the two people that claimed to take responsibility for it where more afraid they were killing the person than helping them - someone else in the family took action of their own.*

*I was told this person had their son quietly step on the oxygen tube, leading into the bedroom, to reduce the amount of oxygen so the person would pass faster. When that did not seem to work well or quickly enough, they disconnected it all together.*

*Of course I was not there. I cannot truly say I actually know what happened. Though there waged a battle for life those hours amongst people that did not know how to discern their own issues from another's. They were not able to hold space for each other or the person in their charge, trying to resolve the last conflicts of his current life.*

This is indeed is an outrageous learning experience for me in holding space for others never mind for the passing of another.

My first comment to Kevin upon learning these new facts was to never ever allow people like this around me if I am on my death bed. I would prefer to be dying alone out in the woods than to empathically or physically deal with such abuse of others not willing to deal with their own issues and lost within their Ego, Opinions, Personality and Learned Knowledge of what is.

I stated within a rush of emotion that "Using a pillow over the face would be a much more humane way to treat a person than what was done."

I am so thankful for what spirit teaches me when I can emotionally overcome myself.

The reasons why I chose to tell this story is not to lay blame or to judge people. It is to tell an honest story of what I have myself witnessed. To explain and show how crucial it is that during the death of another we put aside our own issues.

We need to disconnect from misbelieving it is all about us. Learning to hold the proper space for that person in their own miraculous journey of life and the passing on to an afterlife is crucial. That "after life" is more alive in the higher dimensions than we tend to accept or fathom within the lower dimensions while we are lost within our unresolved issues of not being.

It helps to raise our vibrations and awareness with unconditional love and compassion. While holding out thankfulness and gratitude for being able to be part of the person's life here on earth. Offering forgiveness for anything that is needed helps the person move onwards from any darkness and fear they may have been struggling with.

We can learn to understand the possibilities of past lives. In doing so we gain actual faith in the source of all being to see and comprehend that we do not die at all. The concept of death is only a 3$^{rd}$ dimensional illusion of a play of light that many are lost within repeating till their ascension.

**The Hawaiian Mantra Prayer:**
**"Ho'oponopono" is a helpful tool to work with**

*Try saying this with all the compassion and honesty you can muster while becoming present*

*I Am Sorry,*

*Please Forgive ME,*

*I Love You,*

*Thank You.*

This technique can be used with no particular reason in mind nor directed at anyone but the space in front or within you and still have miraculous results.

Also try directing it to a person you would like to foster a healthier relationship with. (They do not need to be present, nor do they need to be currently alive in physical form) Over time see how your relationship shifts and evolves.

**It doesn't matter "who was right or wrong, or who should be forgiving who" the gift of this is the love and compassion that unfolds from working with it.**

### *My story of working with it:*

*I started using this technique and trying it in several ways. I watched it on 'YouTube' in videos offered with pretty music and feeling surprising emotions well up and shift within me.*

I started doing this as I had clients lying on the therapy table in front of me. While I was offering to hold the space of Reiki I was also quietly within my being and spirit chanting this over and over to them and their spirit.

I offered it quietly from within while people sat or stood in front of me. I then witnessed as they wondered out loud why they felt so much love flow thru them.

I offered it to the higher realms within meditations, to god, to Yeshua, to whoever "up there" could hear me.

**And then one day as I was sitting quietly with nothing in mind**

From the back of me I felt Archangel Michael (who I often feel behind me as if a protective force) swirl to the front of me on bended knees and offer it to me.

Then it felt like what might be my twin, that was never born into this life, who I will discuss in a later chapter, came from within me and offered it to me.

**And then..........**

I saw Yeshua come forth on bended knees, and offer it to me, as I sat and cried and felt the immense realization that came with his message of love.

**I Am Sorry,**

**Please Forgive ME,**

**I Love You,**

**Thank You.**

# The Holistic Center Inc

**THC stands for**

**"The Holistic Center"**

*After my first Reiki attunement I started practicing daily working on discerning those energies. I actually started practicing working with people as clients. Nonpaying clients at first, but they were strangers and clients none the less.*

I would not advise anyone to do what I did in that way. I suggest to students that they get to level 2 of the Reiki degrees and work with it for at least a year before they take clients. Understanding what you are in for in working with people in this manner is important.

*My first teacher told me I was already attuned to Reiki and to a higher level than the first level which she had attuned me to start with. Things like this always added to my curiosity as to when and where did I actually start learning Reiki to begin with.*

*I often say when learning Reiki you need to "practice" Reiki but you do not need to have a "Reiki Practice".*

People are often confused thinking that if you learn Reiki then that means you need to make it into a business. In reality learning Reiki is about working with the energies for our own being. Not because we then need to go fix others.

Just learning to discern the space of "being" to hold space for Reiki to flow is in of itself enough. The best we can do for others in life is to learn to hold our own space and light of being. The more we can do that, the more that itself holds space for others and shows forth light. I believe bringing forth the clear essence of our being is a force of love that allows all to heal within its path.

In no way does that mean we shouldn't help others or offer Reiki to others or even create a business with a "Reiki practice".

**It is all about the intent of what we are doing that matters.**

I have known people to learn Reiki because they felt they needed to "heal" others. It was their prophetic calling and they always seem to be running faster with their "doing" than their being. They trip over themselves in that process. Needing to help others out of our own lack of self-worth or due to issues of ego can be dangerous for everyone concerned. If you need to be a "healer" you then are creating a space so people need to be healed.

I try to caution students to learn Reiki for themselves. If a potential student seems determined that they are to be a "healer" of others, but will not take the patience to heal themselves, I let them know I am not the right teacher for them.

In the end the only thing we can do is heal ourselves with the help of divine guidance since we really cannot heal another. We can hold the space for another to heal with their will and the power of Reiki and spirit and our guidance. It is up to one's own free will if they will work with whatever their processes are that need to be resolved for a true healing to occur.

> *I jumped right into working with people, not out of need, but rather that it was what it was. I was determined to move past the years of darkness. I was seeing a light again and people started to respond to my talk of this new energy therapy I was working with on myself. I said yes to everyone that asked if I could show them what it was all about.*

*I hadn't yet worked with it enough to be able to create all the safe boundaries I really needed for myself. People kept asking for more sessions and I was enjoying most of the experiences.*

*Some people were difficult to experience. It seemed at times I needed to be careful that whatever their issues where, that it didn't somehow become my issue.*

**I hadn't learned about the Reiki symbols at this point like I would years later. Now I realize why it is so important to work with those symbols.**

*I heard in the beginning, from various teachers and students locally, that you really didn't need to remember the symbols or work with them. They claimed since they were attuned to you that was all you needed.*

*I later learned that indeed you do need to learn the symbols. Learning how to work with the Reiki symbols is actually part of Reiki and being able to create and hold the space to work within.*

*There were many things I learned later that would have helped me greatly in the beginning. It would have allowed Reiki to flow much smoother. I would become clearer in the process.*

*I used all my design experience to create a very comfortable therapy room. As my client base grew I took over the whole top floor of the house for my practice. Kevin enjoyed remodeling the entry way for me to make a proper waiting room as well.*

*I knew this was what I would now do. This someday was going to be what helped me become self-sufficient. I knew once I practiced enough I would be able to start charging a fee for the service. I wasn't concerned how and when it would take place for my sight was set on the fact I knew it would.*

*I foresaw that it was going to be much larger than I could even realize at that point. I just needed to learn to hold the proper space for this. It was much bigger than I was since; in fact, it was not about me at all.*

*I started to go to some workshops and enjoyed going to all the types of "alternative stores" I could find. – From Wiccan to Goddess to New Age and Holistic type stores I was experiencing them all. I was discovering various "energy tools" and also crystals and gemstones. I was amazed I hadn't had a passion for them before now.*

*The energies in the stores were interesting to learn to discern. To discover what I felt most comfortable with. I met more people that I could communicate with, regarding the fact I had visions and was an empath.*

I learned much from what didn't feel right to me during this process of interacting with others. While I knew I myself was far from perfect, I learned from other people's issues. I knew that I would not hide my issues but work through them even if that meant right in front of people.

I did not want to be part of some of the things I saw going on at other places that did not feel safe to me.

*One of the places, I was going to with a friend, held space for people to awaken their psychic abilities. It was not a store and their events where small and by invitation.*

*I learned much about holding space for others by their lack of holding space. I witnessed things there that my friend and I were mortified by.*

*In the end I had to stop going to the classes I was taking because of the things I was seeing happen. It seemed to me like very bad guidance to others.*

*The last thing that happened, that I decided I could not ignore anymore, was when two people met at the group and where told the reason they felt they knew each other was from a past life.*

*They were told the attraction they had for each other was from a relationship that was unresolved. It was suggested that if they felt they needed to pick up that "sexual" relationship again, they should. They were told even though they were both married to other people and had families of their own, that they should do this even if their current partners would object.*

*They were told not to tell them. They were told to do it behind their backs. All this was told to them as in "Spirit tells me to tell you this and that it is okay to do so".*

*I was told later by someone, who still went to the class, that when others asked why I suddenly stopped going without any notice that they were told that "He is not ready yet to awaken."*

*I am not sure who the spirit was that told them to give that guidance and I don't think I want to actually know.*

*There was much more that happened which I will not go into as well. Pretty much every one of those people from the class called me out of psychological distress for advice due to the things they were being told. I then realized I needed to do something.*

*I realized I needed to open the space of my practice so that people had a place to come that was safe to share. I started hosting meditation circles and then drum circles.*

*Soon after, people started asking if I would start offering various products including crystals and gemstones. Since I loved shopping at stores that had that sort of stuff I figured I might as well start offering those products as well. With the financial help of friends we created The Holistic Center.*

**I deepened my Reiki training taking classes from many teachers. I went to Winchester Hospital to learn Clinical Hypnotherapy and even took classes to be certified as a Reflexologist.**

*We purchased a bio-sensor machine that would actually show a person's energy fields and aura to teach people that indeed they were made up of many vortices of energy. I would explain in many ways that if they paid close enough attention they would realize that it was a reflection of their spirit they were looking at on the computer screen.*

*I started paying more attention, higher up to spirit, within my meditations and was shown and taught much from the higher spirit realm.*

*I was invited to be interviewed on a few radio shows, then started to be invited back more often. I was terrified of speaking live on air and discussing all the things I had hidden for so long regarding my senses.*

*I realized it was therapy for myself and continued. Then I realized it was therapy for others, even with my issues of speaking.*

**An older man confides in me:**

*Then came the night I was in Worcester, Massachusetts, at a radio station, taking part in a live broadcast with a small in-studio audience.*

*When I finished the show an older man, who looked like he could be the father of some nice family, came up to me and in hushed quiet whispers confessed something to me I will never forget.*

*He stated that he had no idea who I was before I started talking on the radio. He said he was there that night to listen to his friend that was on before me but he felt he would stay for the whole show and listen.*

*Never in his life before had he confessed, what he was about to tell me he stated in whispers.*

*He said he had always heard and seen things, such as I was describing and talking about, live on air, for anyone else to hear.*

*Yet, he quietly confessed to me while inches from my face that his entire life he kept it to himself and quietly figured he was insane.*

It didn't take long for me to know I needed to never worry about speaking of the things I have dealt with my entire life. For there are many others, out there, that need to hear they are not insane.

Soon after I was offered my own weekly hour spot on a local radio station and created "Conversations with Keith" a talk radio show.

In the direction I was heading all I wanted was to create a healthy community to live within. I would make various attempts at creatively bringing people together to form circles of intention.

I dreamed of the day I could expand The Holistic Center into a small retreat center. I dreamed of the possibilities of hosting larger events on an expanded property. People could come and stay or even possibly live with us as we all learned from the space we held for each other.

**Keith at a pottery class**

## Glastonbury is calling

I keep getting drawn to go to England. I have gone each summer the last two years, and have another retreat planned to lead, within the spring of 2013, which we are calling 'The Castle Quest of King James'.

**The Chalice Well Gardens**

The first trip was to go to a Karuna ® Reiki training retreat with William Lee Rand which was held in Glastonbury, England. I made plans to land at Heathrow Airport in London and visit with a friend I had met at a Reiki Retreat in New York the year previous. We planned to then travel to Glastonbury for the training, and then back to London for a few more days of sightseeing.

William Rand suggested reading several books on Glastonbury and its history. Though with everything involved with running The Holistic Center I did not find or make the time to get the books about the area I was going to visit in all the excitement.

That fact of not learning about the area turned out to be possibly guided more by spirit than by my own doing. When I got to Glastonbury I started to have visions on the history of the area. I received clairaudient messages from various spirits regarding what appeared to be my own past life history being connected to England itself. The connection of England and to what might appear as hidden truths of Christianity to many seemed to come forth as well.

Had I read all the books I would have most likely cast off most of the visions and clairaudient messages as elaborations of my mind. I would not have sensed the actual messages with meanings, which I would learn to discern the real meanings of later.

Those meanings keep unfolding with their messages. Like huge sections of puzzle pieces all refitting into the spectrum of my mind's eye showing me much more with each sacred find.

> In Glastonbury we stayed at 'The Abbey House' which is directly on the property of the old ruins of one of England's most treasured connections to what many believe to be the true history of Christianity – The Glastonbury Abbey.
>
> It is said that Jesus as a child traveled to England with his uncle Joseph of Arimathea. Joseph owned rights to tin mines in England and Jesus built his first "Waddle" in what would later become known as Glastonbury, and in fact, on the same property as The Glastonbury Abbey.
>
> Tales say that King Arthur was found dead next to the Abbey and was then buried within it before he was moved many years later.
>
> It is also claimed that Joseph of Arimathea was buried there as well and with him two vials that contained the blood of Jesus Christ.
>
> It is claimed that Joseph of Arimathea was later moved to another church in England - though, what happened to the vials, if they did truly exist, are a secret within history.
>
> While working with Reiki and meditating on the property I would have many flashes of what appeared to be English history.

### I went to "The Chalice Well Gardens"
*(see link at end of this book for more info on The Chalice Well)*

*Very loudly within my mind I heard that a certain spirit wanted to speak to me. I was surprised that I was being asked to grant permission to her to be spoken to.*

*I walked into a certain area of the gardens and realized I should have brought flowers. I kept hearing in my mind earlier in the day that I needed to pick up flowers for someone - and yet did not do it. It did not make sense to me at the time. I then realized the flowers I was sensing I should purchase, were for this spirit.*

*It would have been an offering of respect from me to her and indeed she was waiting to speak with me there.*

*My direct thought was concern if I was making all I was hearing up. I did not know how I could be putting together the information I was hearing since I did not know about these things beforehand. The way it came together told me even more about the truths of what I was sensing.*

*I was concerned with the depth of the information since it was so large. It seemed to pertain to how I was personally connected to Jesus himself. I was told tales regarding Joseph of Arimathea and it would appear there was more than I could handle hearing all at once.*

*I pushed away consciously some of what I was hearing since it was larger than I was comfortable with at the time. How could all this be real?*

*I would later learn much more about those connections and why I was hearing these things.*

We visited Stonehenge and I really have to say, I was not impressed at first. I walked up to the stones and did not feel connected to them. I did not sense much sacred energy. In fact all I could think of was a wall of modern history on them as if blocking me from sensing anything deeper than a one dimensional awareness of a post card setting.

We had registered to have private time within the circle of the stones after closing time and that would be where we would have our last energetic attunements to Karuna ® Reiki.

**Not at all impressed with the stones or the site I took some time to go in the gift shop and buy a few items.**

I was drawn to a couple picture books of Stonehenge which showed a pictorial history. Then what I had felt all made sense to me. I indeed was sensing the modern history of the place and how the stones were impacted energetically and physically by generations of people that did not pay homage or have knowledge to their actual purpose.

Then the time came and we were instructed that we could go inside the circle of stones but could not touch them. I, as most others, took off my shoes and socks to at least touch the earth around them and connect to the energy.

As we sat in our circle within the circle of stones meditating and receiving The Karuna ® Reiki attunements I became very aware of the sacred energy there.

I sensed a huge amount of white light spirit energy and started to feel the presence of Druids around us. It felt strongly like the Druids were aware of our presence there and what we were doing.

*I could not tell if I was seeing into the past history of the Druids. Were they noticing us there from the future? Or possibly they had come from the spirit realm not from the past? Maybe the space of energy I was seeing into was the eternal presence of now.*

*During my trip back to London, with my friend Mirriam, I spent a little over an hour at Westminster Abbey. I just happened by the place, though it felt more like it happened by me afterwards.*

*It was just before closing, so I could only stay till then. The experience affected my life more than I realized or could comprehend at the time.*

*Looking at the entrance, that I went within, I just had to stop several times in awe and struck by an awareness that I did not comprehend. Entering inside I needed to sit for a while to just absorb and settle with all I was feeling.*

*Westminster Abbey is home of many of the tombs of English Royalty and select historically famous peoples. I walked around the tombs dumbfounded by the majesty of the place feeling somehow as if I was home in some strange way.*

> **The building itself seemed like it was part of me, or I was part of it.**
>
> *I walked in awe and within myself started to hear strange things with my emotions. I kept having to push away the feeling if I looked close enough I would find my tomb there. If I was very careful I might find the burial places of two of my lovers.*
>
> *I was confused by my random silliness and desire to let go and just feel those feelings as if they were true facts. I kept stuffing the emotions and pushing away the words I heard within my mind asking me to look closer at where I actually was, and the possibility of whom I actually was.*
>
> **The emotional drama of all this was still hard for me to fathom. I found various ways to push away from it and lose my awareness in other things.**

I would go back the next year and spend my entire trip in Glastonbury, with Mirriam and a couple others, on a retreat that I created and led.

We stayed at 'The Chalice Well Gardens' within little 'St. Michaels' house and vowed to come back again when we could. I called the retreat 'The Vessel Holders of Glastonbury 2011' and that we did. We worked and learned how to be vessels of light and to hold the space of light for each other on each of our own individual quests during the trip.

> *By then I had already worked through many of the things I had sensed and heard from the past years trip. I better understood the connection it seemed I had with Joseph of Arimathea and Jesus. I was experiencing what seemed like past life visions of those times.*

*Jesus, or Yeshua as I better resonated with, would appear out of nowhere in the midst of my day doing things. I would see what would appear to be things happening through the eyes of whom, it seemed I, may have been in that life including with Yeshua speaking directly to me.*

*Then other times I would have visions which seemed like I was being in-tune with others from the time period. I would see and feel and often times hear what they went through.*

*On the flight over the ocean, going back home the air turbulence would gently rock me into visions. I would start seeing/being in-tune with someone covered in robes holding a large staff. There was a semicircle in front of him of three women. They were gently rocking in-tune with the waves of the ocean from deep within an old boat on what felt like a very long voyage.*

*The rocking of my spirit from deep within and the rocking back and forth of those three women and that man all entranced within spirit. All connected energetically and spiritually within a sacred prayer of being.*

**Keith flying over the Atlantic**

*On another flight, over the same ocean, during the rocking of the turbulence I suddenly found myself in the same space with the same women and the man in the robes. Though, this time I suddenly felt sick. I was more aware as if I was being conscious of the woman on the left, of the other two, which would put her on the right of the man in the robes.*

*I was surprised as to why I would be sensing her. Why she was sick? Then just as fast as I encountered those curiosities I realized I/she did not feel sick anymore but was actually holding a baby and that she had just given birth.*

*If past lives are real and if indeed what I have been sensing as to who I was in that time period was true. Then I would have been in-tune with those people on their voyage. I would have helped to pray them to safety, for I possibly was the person that helped them escape to go on that long voyage for to begin with.*

*Or could there be another reason, another deeper layer I did not understand yet – another reason that would explain much more to me in the future.*

I can say confidently that Jesus – or as I said earlier the energy that I know more as Yeshua has taught me much in the last few years within the awakening of my spirit by going within. He has graced me with the ability of being born again within spirit. He seems to be teaching me that reincarnation, if indeed it is real, is part of the whole understanding of being born again. It appears as well that possibly he was not teaching a "religion" as some would imply.

I have had others tell me of visions they have had of Jesus. While I know others that do indeed have visions of him, sometimes I am surprised by the very casualness of what some people will tell me as are their experiences with him.

Some of those experiences I hear make me wonder if they are having visions of their projections of whom they wish him to be, or who they believe he is other than visions actually of him.

During any visions I have had they tend to be so large that it is like a ball of energy that unfolds and awakens everything within my consciousness. It does so without going against my free will and there is a state of total unconditional love with no judgment at all.

I do not understand people that believe in higher powers or Jesus, for that matter, that then judge or condemn others. The only way I can make sense of that is to realize that they actually do not have faith.

What they believe to be their faith is essentially a reaction with judgment and hatred due to the fact deep down they know they do not have faith. They know that they themselves are the ones with the issues. Since they will not allow themselves to deal with their issues they project them off to others as if it is the others issue. That mirroring they see back is what they strike out at and wage wars over.

I have great sadness for those that I have met in life that have told me they do not believe in religion or spirit or god because of what they have seen others do in the name of a religion or god.

I don't think Yeshua believed in that sort of religion either.

Free will is precious and sacred. We have no right to take it away or abuse the free will of others even if it is to try to get them to see truth and light.

The more we go within and align with our truths to allow our spirit to break free in life the more the light can shine through. That act of being can hold the presence of god within and show empowerment of holding the space of presence.

**Ruins of 'The Glastonbury Abbey' - Glastonbury, England**

# Run Away out West

During that vision as a child of five years old, so long ago within this life, I have often pondered on something that was said to me.

I looked away often, during the vision in deep pain. During what I was witnessing and thru-out the vision the man kept saying to me that I needed to run away, that I needed to run away out west.

> *As a small child all I could think then as I heard him say it to me was how can a little boy run away? I didn't have the money to go out west. I didn't have the money to even be able to buy my own food to feed myself how could I run away and survive.*

It made no sense to me at the time. For many years it made no sense. I started to realize one day that I was running away each time I could. Each time I could find the money or the ability I was running away out west. I was running away to Sedona Arizona.

It made no sense till that little boy grew up, but as well it made no sense till the little boy inside of me grew up with me.


***Visions of Dead Ends....***

> *I was driving back to the place I was staying at on a trip to Sedona Arizona. I kept going down a dead end street and needed to turn around and try to find the correct street I was looking for.*

*I was upset that evening. I had a long day of dealing with other peoples issues. They felt threatened due to the fact I was offering aura readings at the same place they were offering psychic readings.*

*They felt in competition with me and created a negative space to work from.*

*Right before one of the incidents of getting a power play pushed at me I sensed what seemed/sounded like one of my mentors telepathically tell me to be careful. I was told in a few moments a woman would come up to me and do something and I needed to be ready for it.*

*I commented about it to the "psychic" who was sitting next to me and he bolted from his seat and walked away.*

*In walked the woman that I was warned about telepathically, and I witnessed the scene I was told about.*

*I found out later that the psychic I was sitting with actually had emailed my mentor before this telepathic experience. He complained about the fact that I was working there that day and potentially taking away any business he might get.*

*He was told in the past that during the busy season there should be two psychics working regardless. It was mentioned that the business was not about competition. It was about offering options during busy periods. People could go to the person that they gravitated to and needed to get help from rather than it being a competition.*

In this line of work a client often is guided to go to a particular person to interact with for the messages or healings that they can manifest within that space. It is regarding alchemy not competition. It is not even about a business concept nor may it be about the person offering to hold the space.

I feel true survival is about learning how to be in the space you are in and how that manifests the flow of abundance or lack of thereof to us. Any expressions of fear only get in the way and create obstacles for the energy of abundance and flow to move through.

**Back to the vision –**

> *I was on that same wrong road that was a dead end. I turned around, went back to the road I knew and tried again. I did this three times and then as my frustration peaked I realized I was living through a vision I had from earlier in my life.*
>
> *I was sitting in the car looking through the rear view mirror out the back of the pickup and realized this was the spot I saw in that vision as a child. I saw the same confusion and felt the same pain. But I laughed harder than I had in weeks.*
>
> *I now was seeing the vision from the perspective of understanding it from an adult frame of view. I understood why I was out west. I even realized that I was driving an old car a friend graciously allowed me to borrow.*
>
> *When I was a child and saw this vision with the help of a spirit, I was confused as to why I would be out west trying to find my home. As a child I knew I didn't live out west and I had no understanding as to why I would be out there so far away from what I thought home was.*

*I was even more confused as to why I saw that I was so sad during the vision and thought I must have a pretty hard life.*

*In the vision as a child I had seen I was lost far from what as a younger person I considered home to be - driving an old car thinking I must be pretty poor. It was very disturbing to me back then. A future lost out west, poor and alone.*

*I had partially heard spirit try to explain that the car was a friends and I was only borrowing it. I was confused and in pain seeing the vision. I was having a hard time paying attention to the spirit trying to teach me about the vision. It even led me to think that it must be a wife that I really wasn't connected to. I thought I must be in the midst of a divorce. That would have even explained the pillow I saw in the back of the truck.*

*If I wasn't on my way home to her and the feeling of not having the energetic connection as one would expect to have with a wife added to the sense of sadness during the vision for me as a child. It seemed like another vision of future sadness I would have to live through.*

Sedona, its vortexes, and the many friends I have met there have all been major blessings of grace within my life the last few years. I have overcome my fears and embraced awareness during my many trips there. I have worked with amazing therapists from Sedona. It seems I may have even recovered friends and family from past lives as well.

I hope to someday have a home in Sedona that I can leave my clothes at instead of always bringing luggage with me when I go there. I even have day dreamed about someday buying a home and what it would look like. I've considered the colors I would paint the place since I always love to redesign homes in my head to energetically fit what feels right for me.

On one of my trips, a close friend told me I could stay at their house they just moved from, that was on the market for sale. When I arrived I was amazed to realize it was the house from my day dreams that I repainted to my desires.

If it turns out to be the home I bring people to stay at and to help them experience their own Sedona awakenings I do not know. Though, I have within my mind decorated the whole place in the furniture I would, if I could, and I have day dreamed of spending afternoons on the large deck with stretched canvas and paint in hand allowing the energy to paint thru me the bliss I crave for.

> *In the vision at nineteen, that I would later understand as The Violet Flame Awakening, I recall looking at the earth from above. I was seeing into my future and the options on my return as to what I would do to help humanity.*
>
> *I felt I had a responsibility to go back into my body in the $3^{rd}$ dimension and help people overcome all the pain I saw them in. It was part of all the pain I knew I was trying to overcome as well.*
>
> *I was disturbed by the cults I saw from above and how so many people where hypnotized by the illusions that were being created.*
>
> *I realized from high above in dimensions so clear that culture itself was a cult that blinded people from the truths of light and the plights they lived were of their own doing.*
>
> *I commented on how I could come back and help people get out of cults. I saw some visions regarding those desires. I*

> heard concern that I might myself, get lost in the cults I was trying to help people get out of, if I was not careful.
>
> From the view above all the routes out of the horrible situations people were finding themselves in were easily marked and understood from the perspective of the higher dimensions.
>
> I didn't stop to consider as I came back into the lower dimensions I might lose contact with those 'routes of perspective'.
>
> In the higher dimensions I became aware of the realm of demons and entities. I saw how they were effecting humanities connection to its spirit light and was told rather boldly that that realm was not the realm I should fully work within.
>
> I was told that it was a man by the name of John Livingston that did that sort of work and I would meet him in my future and he would become my mentor and I would learn from him to do the things he did.

John Livingston feels like a father to me. I feel safe within his guidance and presence and wish I could have run away out west much earlier and found him long ago. Sessions with him have astounded me on his ability to hold space for others. I could clearly see what I was truly seeing by allowing myself to let go of my fears and seeing what was right in front of me.

> One of the first times I met John for a session I laid down on his couch and as he sat next to me he asked, "What do you see?"

*I thought for a moment and remarked surprised, that I actually saw a shape within my mind's eye. I started describing the colors to it and the different aspects to the shape.*

*Then I commented that I didn't understand why I was seeing what I was seeing. I had lain down on the couch determined with my mind I was going to go into something else – yet all these other images where coming to me.*

*I laid there describing the fact I was now seeing a Native American man. He was dancing and singing in front of me and I saw feathers in his hair. Yet, I was resisting on telling about the feathers for some reason, as if I was making this all up, and just had to add feathers to his hair.*

*We then went on to other things in the session. I was amazed at the space John held for me and what he allowed me to overcome.*

*Later that night my friend Laurelle and her husband Michael invited me and a bunch of other people to go to the "Sedona Creative Life Center" for a concert.*

*I sat down amongst all these wonderful people that felt like family. I looked up and was amazed. Directly in front of me, on the stage was the logo for the "Sedona Creative Life Center" and it was exactly what I had seen earlier in the day in my vision.*

*Before I could even turn to comment to anyone my surprise out onto the stage walked a Native American man with feathers in his hair. He started singing while tears streamed down my face. I sat there and realized how amazingly alive I truly was.*

I will offer one more story of an experience with John Livingston. Then, in the next chapter I will discuss one of the most shocking visions I have had in the past twenty years.

This story tells of something that has always been within the back of my mind as to why I always felt like I had a twin brother. Yet no one knew about it.

> *I was planning another trip to Sedona and was looking forward to all the sessions and experiences I would be able to have with my various teachers and mystic friends.*
>
> *Two months before the visit I was sitting at my computer doing some work and suddenly started to feel like I couldn't breathe clearly. I always have been aware that I don't breathe enough at times and I find myself short of breath often.*
>
> *Though, this time was strange. I was seeing something also. As I was having the feeling of being at a loss for breath - I was feeling as if I was inside my mother's womb - and I was a baby!*
>
> *I took a deep breath and thought to myself WOW, now that is something I need to look into. It was the first time that I could recall that I regressed to the womb. I regressed and it was spontaneous and not something I was coached to happen.*

I wanted to share the experience with my mom. Though, I was concerned that she would think I was implying that it might have been her fault that I couldn't breathe well. I chose not to say anything to protect her feelings but shared the experience with close friends.

My mother was finally coming back to more of the consciousness of who she really was. She was finally learning to see that she could remove herself from all the prisons in life that she was in before.

She was learning that other people's reactions were not her responsibilities. Other people's attitude had nothing to do with her. She was finding strength inside so that she could forgive herself for the fact, she had to grow up and learn at the same time as raising children. The children inside of her were still learning to grow up from not having parents to hold safe space for her as she was learning how to raise children.

> *When I arrived in Sedona, at my appointment with John Livingston I mentioned the experience. I mentioned how I've always felt like I was blocking knowledge or awareness of something that happened within the womb before I was born that I was still having a hard time dealing with.*
>
> *John quickly asked if I wanted to go back there and see –*
>
> *Without any prompting from John since he and the angels that work with him already where holding clear space for me to see – I saw it all again.*
>
> *Instantly it was as if I was in the womb again. I realized right away what it was I have been blocking from my emotions my whole life. I was not able to deal with the fact that I had a twin brother. He passed on within the womb while I was there with him.*
>
> *From the very beginning of this current life I have been in trauma from the loss of my twin brother that I would never be able to grow up with; to play with, to learn and*

experience the three dimensional lives that we find ourselves in.

I saw and felt the pain of consciously knowing his body would not grow any more. Our plans of sharing a life together would not be in physical form. The pain of having to continue to grow and to literally will myself to live and be born was traumatizing to me.

I witnessed the interactions of the spirit realm trying to protect my birth.

They cautioned me that I needed to go on. I was allowed to not be fully within the body at times due to the pain of the experience. I knew that I had to absorb parts of his being and $3^{rd}$ dimensional physical material so that I could go onwards.

Towards the end, it was demanded of me to have to stay in body. I needed to be able to survive the birth. The new 'baby consciousness' could not go back into the arms of spirit anymore but had to stay put in the womb to be born.

The space that John and the angels held for me allowed me to realize my twin brother freely gave up his life. He gave up his turn this time at being reborn with me, so that I would be able to live and be born. I realized that he (who has no name within this life) has been a spirit guide of mine my whole life.

**I instantly realized a vision I had many years ago of a spirit speaking about his love for me was indeed him.**

> During that vision it was like the veils of heaven were pierced. I was shocked as to the emotion I felt from the spirit that seemed to be scolded or warned by another spirit for not helping me more in his guidance. He replied with the depth of his love that he was holding space for me for all the pain and suffering that I had been thru in my life. He was offering me time due to how much love he had for me.
>
> It was as if the emotion of his love caused a ripple through the veils of illusion separating heaven and earth. I saw like a hologram the energy of his love and the energy surrounding back and front of his predicament he found himself in with me.

For privacy reasons I will not go deeper into what he showed me during that vision. I will discuss further the story of my regression back to the womb:

> I realized I could actually "hear" my twin brother speak to me when I was emotionally grounded. He spoke to me of his concern for my (our mother) and how he wanted to make sure if I told her this information she would not be hurt by it, nor would she think it was her fault.
>
> I got a sense from him that we were together in other lives. If I heard him right he told me his name from a very long time ago. He then stated, "Of course that I was" and he mentioned a name that I had been hearing for the last few years now as well.
>
> At some point during all of this I sensed my mother, who was home back in Massachusetts. She came to me spiritually and confessed that she was afraid she was going to die this year. She felt that it was her last year of this life

and that she wanted to make sure I knew before she died how much she loved me. She wanted me to know that she was so very sorry for not being able to be a better mother for me and my brothers and sisters.

I knew I needed to be very careful with all this information. Even though I wanted to share it all with my mother I wanted to make sure it was in her best interest in knowing this.

When I returned home from the trip I spoke with my mother. She blurted out before I could really say anything to her that she was used to all the trips I was taking and even though she missed me during them she was fine with them. But this trip was so very different than all the others.

My mother went on telling me how she was concerned that this was her last year of being alive. She felt that she would die this year. I spoke to her about how sometimes when we get older we have good weeks and bad weeks. It just seems as we are older that the bad weeks have more of an impact on us. We need to stay positive and allow life and light into our lives and things will work out well for us.

I knew she was also concerned due to the fact her 75$^{th}$ birthday was coming up and is December 21 – which for many is the end of the Mayan calendar. Many people have lost themselves in fear due to their confusions as to what 'The Mayan Calendar' means.

I went on telling her how much I knew she loved me. I told her that I did not hold any blame for things within my life and I knew how hard of a childhood she endured. I understood and loved her more than I thought she was capable of comprehending and I didn't want her to take that as in insult. But my love for her was unconditional.

She blurted out that the strangest thing happened while I was away. On that past Saturday (the day of my regression) she all of a sudden felt as if I was inside of her again!

At that point, I thought that 'here goes, I am telling her everything – spirit just gave me the okay from that comment.'

I told her the story. I explained how much my twin brother cared for her and wanted her to not think any of it was her fault. I discussed how amazing life is and that we need to allow more light in to feel all the love that there really is. I told her how we never really 'end' and there is no such thing as death and nothing to fear.

My mother was excited and happy to hear the story. She was totally amazed how she literally felt me inside of her during the regression experience, even though she was on the other side of the country. She exclaimed how amazing god and life were.

She went on to tell me things about my birth (some things she had mentioned in the past as well) how the doctor who was so young and handsome spent the night sitting next to her. He held her hand and promised he would not leave her side till she gave birth. I sat and wondered if he was actually an angel but she didn't realize that fact.

She exclaimed how she had always thought that it was an odd thing. No doctor with any of her other births treated her like that. She had never heard of another doctor doing that for another lady. She wondered if there were things going on that they didn't tell her at the time.

**I hadn't yet told my mother about the spontaneous regression two months prior.**

The next day my mother called excited to tell me she was remembering other things. She started to tell me about how right before the birth she was told she needed to put oxygen tubes on. She said that it frightened her since the only time she had seen someone in the hospital with oxygen on was when my aunt died of cancer. She was afraid that they were not telling her that her life was in danger.

She went on to explain they told her that 'her baby' was experiencing a rather difficult time breathing and needed the oxygen to breathe.

At that I was shocked. It was even more of a confirmation to me that all this was actually real and not some sort of played out psychosis I was dealing with.

**Keith and his mother Helen**

# Past Lives Becoming Present Life

*On the way to the "Shamanic Breath Work Session" my new friend Maia and I stopped at a local grocery store to pick up lunch for the afternoon. On the way out of the store we encountered one of her friends named "Maya" and stopped to speak with her for a moment.*

*Maya was looking at me in a very interesting way and I knew she was seeing something as her eyes became more open and very clear; the whites of her eyes just seemed to sparkle with clarity.*

*I asked Maya what she was seeing, stating I could tell from her gaze that she was seeing something out of the ordinary. I was curious if she was seeing one of my spirit guides.*

*Though I somehow sensed it was more within me she was looking at. Maya went on to say some pretty amazing things as to who she saw "that I really was" as she stated.*

*She didn't say anything about past lives. Nor did she say anything that I could call definitive other than grandiose exclamations around the fact that "I was much larger than anyone in Sedona and that I was bigger than what was going on there". She was genuinely speaking what she felt she saw as truth and was extremely gracious in it.*

*She stated that she was aware that I really wasn't showing who I truly was on the outside to people. When she heard we were on our way to a day - long group Shamanic Breath*

*Workshop she seemed concerned. She did not think I should be opening up so much with a group of strangers. She felt I did not need to do that and I needed to be protective of those I was around and their energies.*

*I observed all this with my friend "Maia" who stood back in shock and said "And I am spending the day with you? Why do I get to?"*

*I told Maya that the workshop was with John Livingston, the author of "Adversaries Walk Among Us" and that I would be very safe. She didn't know who he was and I pondered that it was interesting she would say such gracious and outlandish things about me yet she didn't know John. I considered him to be an amazing man and that was possibly the most connected man that I knew to the higher spirit realm.*

*I was amused by her and on one level I realized how much of an energetic ego trip all those statements sounded like. Though as she spoke I was not surprised at all for some reason as to what she said and I realized how odd that was.*

*I had been saying for a long time now with close friends that I was well aware that I was not really showing forth who I truly am. Since childhood that being of who I am has been in hiding waiting for a time of safety to come out due to what I experienced as a child.*

*With my literal/critical mind I thought seriously she is only seeing the opening I have through me to the light of god. All these references are really not about me but rather that light which I know is possible for **anyone** to open to.*

*I laughed and thought "this is the beginning of a fun day."*

*That day actually turned out to be a day that would open doors within me that would shake the very foundation of my current state of consciousness. To the point it would be as if the doors were blown off their hinges never to be able to be replaced.*

*About an hour or so before it was my turn to lay on the blanket and pillow I brought for my introduction to Shamanic Breath work I realized my breathing was already starting to change. It was if I had already started my session and was being prepped by it.*

*An hour or so before this as I was listening to the workshop facilitators speak. I realized "Maia" that was sitting next to me - who would be my partner during this workshop, was actually the person I was told I would someday meet, several years back from a psychic I knew in Florida.*

*Before I left Massachusetts to go to Sedona a few nights ago I was cleaning out one of my desks that I didn't use very often. I had come across notes from that very session. I recalled I had looked at the note and thought as I was tossing it away "Well this never came true" and then "or at least not yet" I heard echo in my mind. I hadn't met this 'Maia' the note spoke about or her son either.*

*The fact is I was in the process of leaving a couple days later to go to Sedona. I would meet and actually stay in the same house with these people; I was foretold I would meet.*

*That lady Maia was sitting right next to me and was going to be my partner for this workshop. I hadn't realized the connection until just then. I was astounded that the note from the psychic session even had said I would meet her out* west. When I was originally told that I pretty much negated everything I had heard since I hadn't thought back then I would actually be going out west. I was so busy trying to create a future for myself in Massachusetts I couldn't see it.

The negation of that thought those years ago was so strong. Even fully knowing I was in the process of preparing to take another trip back to Sedona, Arizona it did not become clear to me that I was already going out west.

Maia looked at me and said "What?" since she saw the look on my face. I just smiled. I was thinking that there was no need to blind myself by trying to create a future since the future already existed in the energy of right now.

As I started to breath in a rhythmic pattern building up the cycle of breaths inwards and then upwards, I was afraid. I was afraid I wouldn't have an experience to work with. I didn't know where to start with this, and was a little afraid of what may happen.

I put my attention onto the violet flame vision I had while I was nineteen. When I went up into the higher realms and saw through space and time.

I started to remember how hard it was, sensory wise, as I was coming back thru into the third dimension. I realized how physically alone I was then. How no one that I knew back then even realized I had that experience.

I started to feel and realize the depths of the experience I actually had. How psychologically traumatized I was back then and how it affected me for years later with post-traumatic stress.

*I realized I still did not even comprehend the depths of the trauma I had experienced by losing or believing I lost my connection to the spirit realm within the higher dimensions.*

*I felt huge waves of pain rip through me. I started to feel like there was an energetic movement shifting thru my body and consciousness. I heard very clearly within my mind the voice of a female spirit say.*

**"You were many Kings, King James, King Solomon and more, and even a Pharaoh."**

*As I heard the word "Kings" I reacted right away within my consciousness and started to push away. I was not hearing all the names I was being told – I was so overwhelmed with what I was feeling my identity did not know what to think.*

*It was apparent she was determined I would hear and understand my being. A lack of understanding the self-worth of my soul would not stand in the way to block the words she would speak.*

*I was hearing a whole list of names of Kings and as I heard "even a Pharaoh" I energetically tried pushing away from it. It just seemed too large and I thought what type of ego trip is this?*

*The dangers for my mind in believing anything of this was reacting thru my consciousness. Even though at the same time memories seemed to flood back to me.*

*I heard the name of the Pharaoh as I was trying to push away from the voice and awareness. Though I heard very loudly as if to make a point "You were the Magnificent*

King" and at that I pushed away inside of myself thinking "Oh my god, why am I experiencing all this."

As I struggled inside and pushed energetically turning away from these thoughts I started to see and feel things, so much so I cannot even consciously at this time pull it all out to discern it all.

It was as if I was seeing it all - yet at the same time forcing it all into my subconscious at the same time. It was too much to behold. Maybe it was just passing thru me or possibly me passing thru it. I saw and felt what seemed like fire. I even felt like I was burning and I could not get away from the feeling. It was like I was succumbing to the universe itself.

I once again saw an image I had seen a few days earlier in a private session with John Livingston. It was an image of a round shape that looked light in color, almost like a full moon that was set into a wave of some sort and then had a long handle on it.

I felt like I was holding this object. But wasn't sure due to the fact my attention was going to the round shape of light. I started to feel as if I was getting drawn and lost into it. As I did it felt like pure energy and it felt like my whole being would be propelled or thrown through space if I continued.

I felt and saw a huge energetic movement move outwards and from within this object. Yet I pulled away from the images out of fear of not being sure what was really going on.

*It felt so real - so in the now. I felt that it was going to happen again just by my ability of connecting to it in that space of now.*

*If this was not a good thing I should not be putting attention into it. Out of fear of not knowing what was going on, I tried pushing away from this scene within me.*

*I energetically felt myself move within my consciousness. I seemed to experience much more. Though I was not consciously able to discern what was going on at the time.*

*I recall hearing those around me, including Maia not sure what to do for me within that space. She started touching me to let me know she was there for me.*

*I recall feeling someone get down on the floor near me. I turned to the energy of that person and realized I was in the fetal position within someone's lap. I just stayed there for what seemed the rest of the session just allowing myself to breathe whichever way my body was allowing and just allowed myself to be.*

*I could feel Maia curl up against and cuddle me from behind. She just stayed there for support totally pressed up against me.*

*As Maia did that at one point I heard her telepathically exclaim "He will not hurt us anymore". I sensed that as she was holding me, she was also within her spirit holding onto her son, that she loves greatly. She was letting him know he was protected as well.*

*As the session ended I realized the other person with me was the workshop facilitator Crystal Dawn. I did not want* to do anything, I was dazed more fully than I can recall in a very long time. I went, was guided to go outside to draw on paper my experience.

I sat outside not sure what to do. I knew there was no real way to represent my experience. So I started to draw with chalk in circles of color like I might do back home, when I paint what I call my chakra/aura paintings.

I sat there feeling like I just became a participant within a mental ward. During the times of sharing our experiences I had to excuse myself several times since I was feeling sick to my stomach. In the end I quietly vomited in the bathroom more than I would have thought possible at that point. I really wasn't sure what to think about what just happened.

I casually mentioned parts of the experience to a couple people I knew, while in Sedona. One person said to me, "The first time I met you I thought you must have been King Solomon in a past life". They then went on to tell me who they thought they were from previous lives.

Another person got quiet and said they could see how I would have been King Solomon. I just sat and thought to myself "Are you not supposed to be telling me this is some sort of archetypal thing and not to take it so literally?"

Three days after the breath work session as I awaited the shuttle to take me to the airport for my flight to take me home, the trip got stranger.

I was waiting for the shuttle at a friend's store "Peace Place", in uptown Sedona. A man stopped in and upon meeting had asked if he knew me.

*I stated I go to Sedona often and possibly we had met before. He then asked me if I was psychic, which thinking we were in Sedona after all I didn't think it was an odd question.*

*I replied that I had visions and heard things all my life. I stated I was becoming aware of what seemed like past lives and that spirit had given me names of some of the supposed lives.*

He started talking about a book he wrote on reincarnation and told me about what he believed were his past lives.

He mentioned some names I had heard before and then even mentioned the name of a Pharaoh.

Then he asked me, "So what are your past lives?"

To which I replied: "Well, I've been told by spirit and have had visions and what seem like memories all my life of what seems to be." I then listed off some of the names but held back on the Pharaoh since he had just told me he believed possibly that he was a Pharaoh in a past life.

It was outrageous, for me to say that I was told I was a Pharaoh in itself - but to make that statement right after him telling me he thought he was a Pharaoh just sounded like I was trying to 'one up' him in some odd way.

When I said spirit told me I was King Solomon he looked at me with more interest and said "It is well known in some reincarnation circles that King Solomon was Pharaoh Amenhotep III in his past life". He then went on and stated, "As I had just said previously that I was 'Akhenaten' in one of my past lives – and Pharaoh Akhenaten was the son of Pharaoh Amenhotep III".

I stood there thinking how Amenhotep III was indeed the name I heard for the Pharaoh that spirit told me I was in a former life. How interesting it is I thought, that I would be told that it is supposedly well known in some reincarnation circles, that he later became King Solomon in another life.

At the same time I realized here I was standing in front of a man that was weaving even more synchronicities into the story and as well might just be my son from another life.

I stood there in front of him as he himself sat in a chair looking up at me in amazement. At forty seven years old and having no children in this life, it suddenly washed over me that this man that was older than me might actually be my son from another life.

He continued to talk and gifted me a copy of his book on reincarnation. He asked if he could call me within a few days after I settle back home.

A day or so later after I returned home he called me on the phone. He asked how I was and if I've had any other recollections while reading his book or researching what I was told where my past lives.

I honestly was a little quiet, since I still was not sure how much I could trust this man. Was telling him everything that transpired in my best interests?

While reading his book I did become aware of many things. I even had insights into what went on behind the scenes while he was writing his book.

*The intrigue continued as we talked on the phone. I sat in front of my computer and quietly "googled" Pharaoh Amenhotep III. As the name came up on the computer screen I saw the exact words I heard in the Shamanic Breath workshop the week prior, when I was told by spirit the list of names.*

**Right in front of me on my computer were the words Pharaoh Amenhotep III ~ The Magnificent King.**

*He was known as The Magnificent King. The same exact words I heard the week prior that had bellowed through my mind. I was trying to push away from the extreme depths of what I was being told by spirit. I was afraid that someone or something was playing a huge game of ego on me. Spirit was determined I would hear the message regardless of when.*

*All the synchronicities were unfolding - all my experience of discerning was working hard to fully understand what was happening.*

For the last few years as I facilitated the teaching, or attempted to facilitate the teaching of Reiki for my students I would often say, "In the end the only thing I am really teaching is discernment for Reiki itself teaches you from within as you work with the blessing that it is."

In my teaching I believe we need to learn to separate and discern Ego, Judgment, Opinion, Personality, and Learned Knowledge to fully be able to hold space. Not only for ourselves as our soul transmits our spirit into the $3^{rd}$ dimensional space that we are in and co manifests our physicality, but also to truly hold space for another.

*After a few deep breaths, I continued looking at the computer screen as my new friend, my possible son from a former life, talked to me.*

*As I scrolled down the article in front of me I saw a photograph of an ancient statue of Queen Tiye the wife of Pharaoh Amenhotep III. Again, I stopped and stared at the realization that the image and the feeling from the image was the same as the feeling that I had gotten the previous month. I had visions of an Egyptian woman that started to come to me within my mind while I was fully awake.*

*On at least two occasions she appeared to me while I was in what I would consider my normal consciousness state and looked at me.*

*In the first experience I saw her walking down what seemed like a corridor or great hall in some sort of Egyptian building. The energy I felt watching her hips sway as she turned to look at me as if she was noticing my attraction to her was as if to say "Are you coming already?" was palatable. The feeling and emotions of her asking if I was going to follow her down the great hall swirled energetically through me.*

*She was gorgeous to me. She had a power and command to her sexuality and sensuality that was blended with what seemed like she was a priestess of some form of divinity.*

*Since coming back from my original trip to England, two years prior, I have had several instances of having what seems like Egyptian Deities give me messages. I even had an experience of an Egyptian symbol energetically pressed into my right palm by spirit during a meditation with William Rand at The Abbey House in Glastonbury, England.*

*I sat at that computer realizing all this. I knew I could only take small amounts of it to integrate at times to grasp better what was going on. I needed to learn to breathe through it all to come to a higher understanding.*

*One of the original times I centered myself to do more research on these names, I was told, found me looking up King James. I thought to myself, well I heard distinctly you were King James – but I thought was that King James I or was there other King James? I reasoned if there are other King James then I would have heard the number.*

*Then I thought to myself it's King James IV! Then countered with NO, King James I and heard again King James IV! Then I countered to myself that if indeed it was King James the IV I would have heard that so it must be King James I and that is what I looked up.*

*In finding King James I, the page on the computer highlighted the fact that he was King James VI of Scotland before he became King James I of England.*

*After seeing this - for two weeks within my mind I had turned the VI into IV and thought I was seeing that King James I of England was also King James IV of Scotland.*

*I thought that was the reason I kept hearing King James IV as well as King James I.*

*The visions and seeming memories of King James I - are very strong for whatever they mean. I would have memories of being a small child dressed in strange clothing with a falcon and then see paintings later that showed that child with the bird.*

*As I became aware of the small boy I would sense major abuse and fear. I would not only sense domination but I would become aware of the pain of sexual abuse as well and feel his traumatized reactions from deep inside of me.*

*I would later read about known facts of the abuse he withstood under the charge of his regent. My mind would wonder as I pushed away the little boys fear and asked it to go to the light to heal who ever this boy was – and what abuse did he suffer. It wouldn't matter to me if indeed I was him. What would matter here was that love needed to replace the fear and pain that was there.*

*There was one last discovery I could look at of the life of King James I – that made me walk away from my computer and not look deeper. It was when I looked into his life at a Castle he lived within and discovered that there is a story about the death of a woman that was considered a witch. At a very young age he had to make decisions regarding things history does not tell regarding her.*

*The thing history does tell is that she is known as "The Mistress of Keith".*

**And then it started happening again –**

*The visions from my childhood of dying on a battlefield started coming back. I started to feel and see and remember while being on horse and dying in a horrible battle. I literally was getting a sense of the field we were within.*

*I started to realize what it seemed I was recalling was indeed the death of King James IV as well as at times the life of King James I – two distinctly different Kings.*

*During that vision of the Shamanic Breath Workshop I was told "You were many Kings."*

*I was told certain names and I heard there were more as well. I had pushed away from the gravity of the fact I was even being given more outrageous names.*

*A couple months later, when telling this story to a close friend, I sat in amazement when I suddenly flashed to a memory of when I was nineteen and had been hospitalized for several months for what was termed a nervous breakdown.*

*I remembered a girl, I had befriended while there, with a very unusual last name. She told me several things regarding the history of her last name and how it dated to ancient times and that most people with that name changed it due to things about the name that I really didn't understand back then.*

*The thing that stood out to me, within this flash of memory, was a day she came back into the hospital to visit me. She handed me a bible that she had gotten for me. As she held onto it and was pressing it into my hands she kept repeating to me "This is your bible, THIS is your bible, this IS YOUR bible" she asked me to always remember that and turned to her parents in heartbroken sadness exclaiming quietly I do not think he understands what I am saying to him.*

*Of course it was a King James Bible -*

*As I continued looking at the computer that initial day of dealing with the possible energies of King James and what was going on I saw that he also was King of France even though it was in name only. He did not have any real control over France from what it seemed.*

*I sat and reflected how strangely all my life I have secretly felt like in some strange way that I never understood that I was supposed to be a King of France. Yet for some reason I was never allowed to be.*

*As crazy as it may sound it is a memory that I have wondered about for many years. Why I loved Fleur di les so much and why I have always felt like there was some inheritance that was being kept from me.*

*During the retreat I led to Glastonbury, England the past summer in 2011 just months before all these past life names were told to me, I actually confessed this strange fact of the sense of loss of the French royalty line. I expressed how it affected me so greatly within a rather dramatic sharing circle with the people that attended my retreat.*

*Of course they all seemed at a loss of comprehending as I broke down sounding rather insane. I actually cried while explaining my feelings and confusion of those hidden thoughts all my life.*

I have always turned these thoughts into just a realization that maybe it only has something to do with being part French in this life. It must be some weird consciousness experience of not feeling like I fit in. I always felt that there is supposed to be more here for me in this life since I know that I have more to offer.

*There are times I consciously have recalled hearing within my consciousness certain spirit voices. They have made comments about the fact that they could never allow me my true inheritance because of what I possibly could or would do with it. I heard them exclaim that it is so much that there is not enough in this physical world to cover it to give it to me.*

**Spirits –**

People often say "spirit" told me – Well, Spirit Who?

Could it be "The Holy Spirit"? Was it your higher spirit? Possibly it is the spirit of your passed on grandmother? What spirit was it?

I've had to learn to discern if I was hearing my own thoughts in my head or maybe another person's imprints of judgments from the past.

Maybe it is a passed on spirit. And then who?

Maybe it is a person still alive but knowingly telepathically communicating with us?

Or maybe it's the neighbors' random thoughts that are all over the place and I keep picking up on them as if I am some sort of receiver with a radio dial that keeps shifting stations. I know I have certainly felt them having sex at times and I know it's real I hear them in my head as well.

I've even had chest pains for most of a weekend several years back as I sat at my desk next to the window of the driveway wondering why I would feel what I did when I was perfectly healthy.

It dawned on me what was going on, when on that Monday I found out my neighbor a few houses away passed from a heart attack. I had often telepathically heard his emotions as it was, I wasn't aware at the time I was feeling his passing on as well.

Possibly it is a higher spirit helping guide me, or a "lower spirit" trying to confuse me with false evidence appearing real to control me and keep me from the truth.

And sometimes it could be a person looking through our aura and energy fields into our future and casting their reactions and opinions into us without even comprehending the implications of the actions of their presence.

**Are past lives real?**

Well, people have lived before us.

But all joking aside - have we ourselves lived those lives and are products of reincarnation?

What do you think?

I know I keep having flash backs and what appear to be memories of other lives. Am I seeing into lives I have had or I am I seeing into the lives of others?

I am meeting people and becoming aware of who I think they were in other lives and as I quietly keep those secrets they start telling me who they always have thought they were. I realize it's the same person I am seeing.

I seem to be meeting my friends and relatives from other lives and "family is coming together once again" within a reunion of the space of time.

Am I seeing into the lives of others to learn through the history of time and humanity?

In coming down from the higher dimensions through the portals of time did I come across and thru the history of Earth and its people collecting memories from those lives that caught my attention?

Are they only archetypal lessons? Are they archetypal for some and real for others?

Are we all ONE and thus we have memories of all the lives that are ours?

**How many Cleopatra's can there be?**

When I started seriously considering what reincarnation might mean in the last few years I kept having people say to me: "Well so many people think they were Cleopatra or some other famous person there can't be more than one of the same person".

Well, that's not actually true – but that might need to go into another book to explain it in detail from my visions.

Some people might think they were Cleopatra due to the energetic imprint she had on them in that life. For example, if their own lives were that repressed to a very quiet hardly existing presence of being and her presence over took them, they might indeed have memories thinking they were her - or they wanted to be her in that life.

And sometimes possibly if it is a life of a 'great soul' that has ascended very high they could have expanded into many bodies on their return. Their soul and shared memories are within multiple living people.

And sometimes possibly one person could have been 'the one and only' of that former life.

Possibly it is just psychosis.

And even stranger possibly in the case of 'walk-ins' that the person which was born to the body had decided within the higher realms within their 'contract' of coming here that they would give their vessel to another soul with the free will to offer a certain purpose to the ascension of Earth and its inhabitants.

Or during their life they decide they cannot go on – or even they have completed what they came here for and then offer their vessel a chance to do more with a spirit who does not have to go through the difficulties of childbirth and can walk in fully aware.

Consider for a moment that some of the confused children being born today feel they are in the wrong bodies. Consider as well that some of those children feel they are supposed to be the opposite sex. What if in some of these cases they spent so many past lives as an opposite sex that when they are reborn now they have a difficult time adjusting to their new path.

How much space can you hold for the life of another without placing your own judgments and opinions as well as limited knowledge obstructing their own path of awareness?

Many believe not only are people ascending, but the planet itself is in a state of ascension within the galaxies. All the great shifts we are seeing within the current age are mirrors of those shifts.

What is important is the NOW of our being.

Is time a figment of imagination and space the holder of all that there is?

We are all much greater than we show ourselves to be. There is no need of pride or ego of past lives of greatness. There is no need for shame or regret for past life sins. There is no need to prove ourselves, for all that does is blocks all that we are.

We are greater than we present ourselves to be when we comprehend the light of the universe. The source itself many call god, by various names is within us, it is us.

So go within and come forward into the time and space of the eternal now for all else blocks your light.

Some say we are gods in the making – no one better than another, no one less than the other. We do not exist without each other and that is a secret key of existence to holding space for another and ourselves.

Come forth and bring your presence of being. There is room at the table for the greatness of who we are. The more light we bring forth to this table of life the more we can see who we are as well. The more we can see each other, the more we remember we are family.

## The Future is NOW

For some time now I have been running away out west to my past and future to a space of the eternal being of now.

It has taken me a lifetime to tell this story within this book, due to the "False Evidence Appearing Real" that has haunted me through my senses.

I had become lost in the pain and suffering of others. I had become lost in the illusions of the psychological constructs of others. I had become lost within the Egos, Judgments, Personalities, Opinions and Learned Knowledge of others as well as my own shadows of those things. In doing so I had become lost within the multidimensional constructs of the coming forward of my own being.

I had risen to the heavens and fallen to the depths of existence.

I have awakened to life once again.

This book is a tribute to life, to that source called by many names god.

This book is a hope that the Awaking Spirit and reclamation of being that is currently taking place in the cosmos and centering within the energetic fields of Earth will be of peace and love for all.

There is no need to bring down holograms of destruction, anger and hatred. There is no need to judge others since that judgment itself judges our own beings.

The energy, the attention we put to things, adds weight and gravity to the holograms above us. What we fill those holograms with is the character and composition of what we bring to us.

We do not need to bring a "second coming" of pain and destruction. We do not need to fulfill prophecies of others. We can let the love of god grace our presence as we go within and come forward.

If indeed past lives are real then we are our ancestors. We are the ones we have been waiting for.

Go within and come forward into the light – there is no need to die to get here.

**There is no need to kill for a god.**

Do you dare claim impotence upon such a supreme force that it cannot take care of what is needed?

Hatred within people is the judgment they have given themselves as they have separated from their source and thus it does kill them. We see the power of god within that space as it has held with free will for others to choose to come to love or not.

**There is a woman that I know –**

*There are times when she is in my presence a veil separates and I see into what appears to be another life.*

*She may be 'idly talking away at me' chattering away at some drama or concern she is working with and I see another woman thru her and she is doing something else.*

*It appears she may be my wife from another life –*

*I see things that shock me to my core during these partings of veils of spirit and what appear to be dimensions within time.*

*I have seemingly held her in my arms in these visions as we are in the roman coliseum with lions all around. I witness her fear and attempt to be strong for me in her faith and awareness of the truth of light and that there is no death.*

*I witness what appears to be her father, crippled and old, angry at me for once again being responsible for the family's predicament.*

*I see the small baby that appears to be thrown as almost if it is a football into the pit with us.*

Life feels much different with depths of holding space. When you learn to stop reacting off things and go within and hold a space of light for all that you are.

Within the space of light there are truths that would stop the presses of the worlds 'news'- I ask you to stop believing the lies of illusion and comprehend the world is full of love.

There are some that wish to take your attention for their own control and needs. I ask you to consider going within, going deeper than you have ever considered before and find your light of love within that light that is unconditional. There is no other love than an unconditional love.

Take care of that light. Foster that light to come alive even more than you comprehend it could. You are far greater than anyone may have dared to tell you before for they had fear of their own.

### I had a vision of Pope John Paul II –

Months ago there was a flash within my vision. It seemed to happen so fast I almost didn't believe it to be real.

Within the flash of light I saw what appeared to be Pope John Paul II.

Much awareness came with the flash of light including other spirits holding space around his spirit.

It took me some time to deal with the reality of what I was being shown.

I have had visions of "Yeshua" who most people call Jesus. I have had visions that seem to show me lives where my spirit itself knew him personally during his physical time on Earth.

Somehow the visions I had of Yeshua, as profound as they are, seemed easier to deal with than these visions of Pope John Paul II.

It took me time to realize, if indeed as a child I could have met the man within the astral realms of visions that would later be known as Pope John Paul II then indeed I could meet him again after he had passed on to those astral realms himself.

The times of connecting with his spirit have not been easy. There were many actual demons in his life that he had to fight and my awareness of their energetic impact on his life's work goes deeper than some might dare suspect.

### *That woman that I know –*

*I have held the space of Reiki for this woman during sessions filled with great love and light.*

*It is as if often as I start the session her spirit already is lifting off to the heavens, the higher dimensions as I energetically catch up to her to help guide her for her needs.*

*During one recent session that started off very dramatically full of veils of light opening many things occurred.*

*Towards the end of the session I stood up and walked to her feet as she lay fully dressed on the therapy table and sat to hold her feet.*

*As I looked at my hands before I placed them on her- I overwhelmingly felt the presence of Pope John Paul II. It was as if his face was lightly covering my face and he started to gently weep within my hands.*

*I became so humbled and unsure of what was transpiring within the space I was holding. Then as I put my hands on her feet I became aware that it was as if I was standing at the feet of Yeshua on the cross.*

*It felt a very familiar place to be.*

*The only difference in the feeling this time was it did not feel of pain.*

*It felt as if a huge wave of awareness came over me that I (we) the spirit realm was offering and sharing the gift of Reiki to Yeshua. The gift of spirit light was being shared to* all. That Yeshua himself was in the glory of that power of light as well and offering it to all.

I sat overwhelmed in bliss and amazement of the possibility that I was offering distance Reiki to my dear friend Yeshua thru time and space.

I realized he was aware of it. His face appeared directly in front of mine as a wave of light and unconditional love.

And as soon as those feelings and visions washed over me I suddenly became aware of a force of life and in way I cannot explain in mere words – I felt Islam come and greet Yeshua himself together within this space of love. It was as if I was seeing a marriage of life in front and inside of me.

I sat in shock immersed in what the heavens were showing me with a wedding of faith. As the images, as the feelings and power merged in wedded life the impact together became what seemed like a dove of light that then manifested into the goddess known as Quan Ying – the goddess of compassion and love.

The spirit of unconditional compassion and love, the spirit of Quan Ying rose above as like a dove and filled the heavens with the love of humanity.

At that exact moment the woman in my care opened her eyes and the music playing softly in the background finished.

It is said that "Quan Ying" stands at the gate of Heaven waiting for the last soul to enter. When she first encountered that gate eons ago she turned and heard the cries of humanity and could not accept to go on further. Her compassion and desire has been to hold the space of unconditional love for all others to help pass thru in their time.

I realize the gravity and the light of this book as well as the field of reactions people may feel the need to take part in if they read or become aware of the material.

Some friends have suggested I write it under a "pen name" though that made no sense to me. I will not live with fear any more, there is no life in fear.

This book does not say that I am better than anyone. This book does not say I am less than anyone. We are all uniquely different yet we are all part of each other – reflections of light in the universe.

As you discern yourself you learn to discern others.

The reactions of others are not my responsibility. I no longer am a product of other peoples conditioning. If a person fails to comprehend who we are that does not make their miscomprehension out to be who we are.

### My friend Laurelle Gaia –

*A long time ago I hid in that barn in North Brookfield, Massachusetts waiting to see what spirit was trying to show me. I saw an image form in the middle of the air of what appeared to be a spirit of a woman and then transform into another woman as well.*

*As I had said earlier, in the chapter it was discussed, that the first spirit I seemed to see appeared to me as the mother of Yeshua, Mary.*

*The first time I met Laurelle in this life at a Reiki Retreat in Hunter, New York I stood and stared at her wondering why I felt I knew her. Why did she already feel like family – why did I have such a deep love for her on the first glance of her presence?*

I would walk up to her to ask a question and see the light and love of Reiki beam thru her eyes. My questions would disappear in thin air for I already had been given the answers.

When I finally sat in circle and listened to her guide a meditation I realized the long lost secret of mine.

When she stated with the full I AM presence of her being: I AM Laurelle Gaia.

I saw back to my childhood and realized that she is who I saw and heard in those moments of confusion.

I do not know if as a child I had looked into my future and pulled forth the vision of that day of her into the thin air of that barn as she stated the "I AM" presence of her being.

I do not know if in that moment of need the mother of Yeshua brought forth the higher spirit of my friend to show me there was someone waiting for me in the future to help guide me back to being.

I do know that as with all great facilitators of teaching they can at times communicate thru the realms of spirit. I do at times hear the voice of Laurelle caution or direct me in things.

*One of the most amusing times of seeing this happen was a couple years ago while I was at Lily Dale, New York.*

*I was getting a psychic reading from Reverend John White – someone whom, I as well, had seen in visions from my childhood that I would meet later in life.*

*John was in the middle of telling me about a man he sensed I was from one of my past lives. He was bringing forth curiosities of my own as well that I always had of this particular man and why I had such a connection to him.*

*In the middle of this psychic reading I started to hear very loudly in my head my friend Laurelle speaking to me as if she had just walked in the room and was standing next to me.*

*She was cautioning me about listening to the information about this particular possibility of lives.*

*As she was talking to me drowning out the voice of Reverend White he excitedly started to change the subject - to tell me that he sensed my mother in the room.*

*He then quickly changed his comment to say, wait NO, your mother has not passed on, and she is not in the spirit realm.*

*But he continued - this is like your mother, this is like a mother, what I am sensing is like GAIA mother earth herself here with you in this room! He became very excited as to what he was sensing and feeling within the room.*

*I sat and laughed, missing some of what I was hearing from the spirit of Gaia in amazement that Reverend White was picking up such accurate information.*

*Within my many healing sessions with Laurelle one of what appears to be my past lives - a life of actually knowing Yeshua in person when he walked this earth in the physical realm seems to almost always come forth to share light.*

*It seems to me that on the higher spirit realm that Laurelle's love of Yeshua wanted to make sure that the possible past life I would pay attention to and learn from would be the one that held the secrets of Yeshua himself.*

There is much more I could tell of what appears to be that life long ago and I am considering doing so, in another book. It seems to me that it will blend in much more information I have yet to speak of.

This book, as is my life, is very much guided by spirit and this book is of spirit.

### **Jesus Christ, Superstar!**

*As a small child living on Orchard Road in North Brookfield, Massachusetts many things happened to me.*

*One of the things that would follow through my early life that I never understood till now was the day my mother brought home the vinyl record album of 'Jesus Christ Superstar'.*

*We all sat in the living room and listened to the music. It was a family gathering with all us kids and was a moment that felt blessed within time.*

*As the song 'I don't know how to love him' started to play I started to cry. I was sitting on the floor a small child of possibly six years old and all I could do was lie on the floor and gently weep as if my soul itself was pouring forth my body and spirit all over the floor.*

*Any time that song would play I would weep uncontrollably for reasons no one in the room would understand.*

*Later in life as an adult, as someone who started to realize certain visions and their meanings who started to realize the possibility that when Jesus "Yeshua" taught Nicodemus about being born again of spirit that he was teaching him about reincarnation. Indeed he was attempting to teach and awaken Nicodemus as to who he was in his past lives as well and his connection to Yeshua himself.*

*I would have visions of Yeshua's Uncle, - Joseph of Arimathea, as well. Spirit would tell me things about him at The Chalice Well in Glastonbury England.*

*Confusion regarding these two men and their connection to me would teach me even more of what seems to be the hidden truth of Christianity itself.*

*As the religion of Christianity formed throughout the ages would the truth of Jesus, even the truth of his real name, become hidden and suppressed in veils of religion formed to actually disempower the truth of what actually happened those many years ago?*

*Is the real "second coming" that so many fear really only the coming of the truth and the letting go of the illusions of who he actually is and what the real teachings are?*

*Is fear of pain and torture of that judgment day only the reactions from the falling away of the old paradigms of false evidence that was made to appear real.*

*Is the only thing holding back the light and truth for the whole planet those that claim a right to manage and control the free will of others as they themselves stand in the way of the light with their false positions of power?*

*Was Christianity actually hijacked from within the church itself to control and manage the masses as opposed to offering them the light of the real message which is unconditional love and the gift of free will?*

*As those holding on to the lies of illusion in fear and lack of faith let go of their managed positions of their lives the demons will lose all power over the masses.*

*The outcome of choosing pain or bliss for their own souls is all within the holograms they wish to empower. It is within their own making of what they bring down to themselves.*

Some may feel the need to empower the holograms of hatred, fear and judgment to make fearful prophecies appear true in the near future.

Those that wish with their freed will, to hold the space of light, will witness that the holograms of destruction do not need to be the holograms that are brought down upon them.

We may have to witness and hold space for those going through an illusion greater than the recorded history of Earth recalls.

If we go within and come forth into the light of unconditional love we may be able to hold the space for those to go within as well. They can see the light of their truths and overcome the false evidence appearing real, so that their fears ascend intuitively towards heaven.

Grace will prevail in unconditional love.

## Om Shanti Gaia

Peace Through Transformation of Fear

## What comes next?

The next few months will be exciting. The next few years and onwards will be an exhilarating space of time as life is coming forth.

I will continue leading retreats with more of them around the world.

I will still work with clients one on one and hold the space of the facilitation of teaching. Though the manners in which I do it will change.

I will write more books and I will create more meditation CDS and other materials.

I will continue to live a life of richness, no matter how wealthy or poor I am in physical finances or if I am in flesh or spirit.


## Will "The Holistic Center" continue?

Will the dream of the community retreat center be born? Those answers can only come within time and if people become more present to take part for it is within their free will to do so or not.

You cannot build a community if people are not willing to come together. You cannot build a community of unconditional love if people are not willing to love unconditionally.

And then parts of me long to become a recluse again – painting and writing – gardening and sitting still in meditation.

## A NOTE OF THANKS:

Thank you for taking the time, for your attention in reading this book. I hope you have gained from your experience. I hope you have gone within and seen more of the light of your own being inside any reactions and emotions from the things you experienced in these pages and within yourself.

While this is an autobiography of memories and experiences of my life I have hoped by conclusion your attention has gone within more to you than me.

This book is a signature of my life and by such, I feel no desire to, "sign autographs" or to be energetically attached to it as it develops a life of its own played out for us to see.

I have grown and I continue to –

I am no better or worse than anyone else. With that said do you fully realize how amazing you actually are?

If not – possibly it is time you did.

### *A moment in time –*

*If you take a moment in time of meeting someone consider looking within their eyes and sharing a moment of BEING love.*

*Handshakes were created to prove one did not have a weapon in hand.*

*Hugs were created to share an embrace of humanity.*

*Standing tall fully in presence shares the light of spirit of us all.*

*May you gain wisdom in your choices of a moment in time.*

KJC

# LINKS

*For future information on this book and workshops relating to this book:*
www.AwakingSpirit.com

*For information regarding Keith J. Chouinard:*
www.KeithChouinard.com

*For information regarding The Holistic Center:*
www.TheHolisticCenter.net

*For information regarding John Livingston:*
www.John-Livingston.com

*For information regarding Reiki on the web:*
**www.Reiki.org** and **www.ChristianReiki.org**

*For information regarding Sedona, Arizona USA:*
www.VisitSedona.com

*For information regarding Glastonbury, England and The Chalice Well*
www.ChaliceWell.org.uk

*For information regarding The Lily Dale Assembly in New York USA:*
www.LilyDaleAssembly.com

Please note: We have no control over the future working of these links on this page but will update as needed in future editions of "Awaking Spirit reclamation of being" and on the books website

Lightning Source UK Ltd.
Milton Keynes UK
UKOW04f1833050515

250935UK00001B/29/P